GROWING SOMEWHERE

Living life after mid-life

... also by Kelly Walker

Books

Loss of Soul: Burnout

Dancing on the Ark: Facing Change in Uncertain Times

Recordings

24/42

Nomad

River Ash

All My Life

GROWING SOMEWHERE

Living life after mid-life

Kelly Walker

KW Productions©

Canadian Cataloguing in Publication Data

Walker, Kelly, 1941–

Growing Somewhere: Living life after mid-life

Includes bibliographical references and index

ISBN 0-9680315-4-4

1. Middle aged persons—Conduct of life.

2. Self-actualization (Psychology) I. Title

Published in Canada by

KW Productions, 1-800-438-3422, www.kwalker.com

Printing

Webcom Limited, Toronto

Cover Concept and Photography

Arabella Pines

Book Design, Editing and Typesetting

Judy Anderson Communications

To Godfrey Schuett and
Marjorie Morgan, elders

To Ruth and Irving Frisch, Dagmar and Gerry Stafl
and Ruby and Dick Spurr, neighbours

To Tom Harpur, Gerry Judd
and Ken Allen, mentors

Kelly Walker cannot stop the music. And he will go out dancing. *Growing Somewhere* has universal life lessons for us all — how to live our autumn years with enthusiasm and grace — encouraging us to "embrace the future with trust, solidarity and conversation…." A very personal account, full of real life stories from real live people who have taken life by the you-know-whats and want us to do the same!

— *Marci Lipman, Entrepreneur*

Contents

We are all in this together.

Alone.

— Jane Wagner

Introduction

It's three a.m. I can't sleep. I have just finished forty- two radiation treatments for prostate cancer. It looks like I'll be fine. I feel as though I am turning a new page again … new beginnings. Somehow, I never thought I'd live to this age …

I remember so clearly the day that the Toronto *Globe and Mail* arrived at the door with the headline reading, *A Bomb*, and then a bit later, *H Bomb*. I remember, as clear as a bell, having bomb practice in elementary school, squatting on the old hardwood floors under our wooden desks, preparing ourselves for the blast. We called it "duck and cover." I remember the bomb sirens that would announce our need to be ready. I remember when the sirens were installed throughout the city. I remember the bomb shelters and the fear of impending doom we lived with. I feared that I would have to join the army one day and be prepared for a violent death … because I was a fit young man.

My stepfather, an avid military man, would shout commands — likely wanting to "play war" with me — while I cowered in utter fear at the harsh tones of his commands. World War II offered him the best years of his life, as it did for many in his generation.

But the eternal hell of a potential World War III offered me nothing but oblivion.

I remember Sister Fleurette having us put our heads on our folded arms on our desks and preparing us for the moment when the Communists would arrive at the door. They would surely ask us to declare our belief in Christ. Would we be brave enough to be martyrs for the faith, or would we give up our faith in order to live?

I never thought I would live to see my fiftieth year.

At the age of twenty, I entered the novitiate of the Dominican Friars in Saint-Hyacinthe, Quebec. It was 1962. The Cuban crisis was in full swing. I remember gathering around the radio in the old monastery with the other friars and listening to the news, awaiting the word that it would all come upon us at any moment.

My grandmother Lettner was related to Rose Fitzgerald Kennedy and so I was even more intent on the news, because I knew my "cousin" Jack might well be the one to push the button first. Soon we would all be dead. I thought that being enclosed in the monastery with the others, rosaries in hand and heads bowed, we would dance into death in peace and in community. I felt safe in my terror.

I have abandoned the thought of death by war or by atomic catastrophe, although they are still constant possibilities … even now. I have gone through fiery gates that made those terrors look like Disneyland.

Most of us have journeyed treacherous paths by the time we reach age fifty. But the new challenges that present themselves to us at this time are no less daunting: cancer, obsolescence, Alzheimer's, widowhood, poverty, incontinence, loneliness, helplessness, boredom.

I felt that on the eve of my release from radiation therapy five years ago, I was once again turning a new page towards a yet uncharted journey. Where would it lead me? I had absolutely no idea. But I did have an inkling that it would lead me somewhere that I had not yet even imagined. Frightening? Yes. But, what the hell, I've done it before.

My story to this point is no different from yours. The colour of the page is different. The typeface is different. But the story is the same. Every human being is called to *grow somewhere*. In the words of Leonard Bernstein, *There's a place for us, somewhere a place for us.*

Where is it? Who knows? We can choose to *go somewhere* or to *sit idly and* be *done unto*. The true challenge for a maturing human being is to *grow somewhere.*

We grow best when there is a *positive somewhere* in sight. With this in mind, I suggest that you begin your journey through this book by starting with the Conclusion following Chapter Five. *Growing somewhere* benefits from having both ends of life in focus at all times. Happy journey!

Kelly Walker,
Ash Croft, in the Hockley Hills, 2005

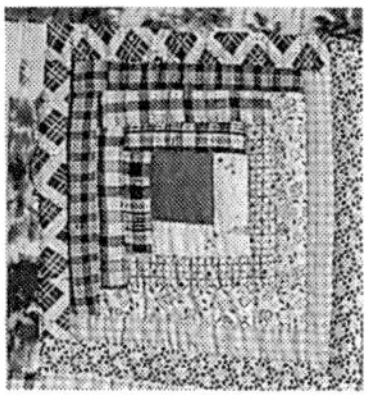

1

Exit or Entrance: How to Position Ourselves for Trust Rather than Despair

> If I can't dance, I don't want to be part of our revolution.
>
> — *Emma Goldman*

The gift of time with which our generation has been honoured is new. Few of our ancestors lived to be very old. But times have changed in the past fifty or so years. As I read over the obituaries in our Toronto newspapers, I realize that the majority of the deceased are now in their eighties and nineties. It is not unusual for someone to have celebrated a hundredth birthday.

We have five birthdays to celebrate this year for family members who are over eighty. In our family, this is the first generation to live that long.

As we forecast our own futures, we are more and

more inclined to think that we will survive to a fine old age.

The best thing about being "over the hill" is that you begin to see the whole picture. The trek to the top was the principal thrust of the first half of life. That goal drove us to do things and go places and dream dreams. It was, after all, the first gift of time for us.

We could describe the periods of our human growth as moments on the journey. Many talk about three major moments in our growth.

The first moment is the one we live from childhood, through our adolescence and into adulthood. It is in this period when we get a primary grasp of ourselves. We live under the umbrella of our elders who help define who we are to be. Often we live our lives as defined by our parents and grandparents, our religious leaders, our governments and the dominant culture. It is, essentially, a period of discovery of self within the universe. Little by little we learn the language of survival and appropriate to ourselves those realities that fuel our being. So much of our life is spent pleasing others in order to be successful (usually someone else's definition of successful). We date, mate and work.

For many of us, it was primarily a journey lived for others. It was a gift given to us from our parents, our society, our friends. But it was a gift with many strings attached. We had hoops to jump through, others' dreams to fulfill. We entered it with all the hues of family scripts — heritage, culture, dreams and faith — and at the same time with all the toxicity that our forbears struggled with. It would become the wallpaper, or the underpainting, upon which we would live our days and nights.

The second moment is unpredictable. Jung says,

> Totally unprepared, we embark on the second half of life. Or are there perhaps colleges for forty- year-olds which prepare them for their coming life and its demands, as the ordinary colleges introduce our young people to the knowledge of the world? No, thoroughly unprepared we take the step into the afternoon of life; worse still, we take this step with the false assumption that our truths and ideals will serve us as hitherto. But we cannot live the afternoon of life according to the program of life's morning: for what in the morning was true will at evening become a lie.

This second moment is sometimes marked by trauma. The journey taken to this point is put under scrutiny. Many aspects are put into doubt. Assumptions that were lived by, beliefs that were wholeheartedly adhered to, relationships that were embraced in the throes of passion and idealism are often radically questioned. Things don't feel as sure and secure any more. Old institutions, mentors, relationships, jobs and attitudes become suspect. Cracks appear in the armour — both of self and of others. The piercing drive towards an authentic self can drive old definitions right off the screen. This is the most difficult period in most of our lives.

It also can serve as the springboard for a marvellous twilight and evening in our life. We have been so ill prepared for the gift of this mid-life journey that most people waste good energy on shame and guilt, unaware that this is the worst and best of times. Out of the many deaths can emerge glorious life. Deaths are required for the true resurrections that the last gift of time can offer.

The third moment. It is within the context of death, I believe, that we can live the last gift of time as a gift. Without the consciousness of death before us, we are inclined to half-live or *pseudo*-live our final years. And in our time, that last period could last as long as thirty or forty years.

We need to *position* ourselves for positive growth during this period. For most of us, mid-life is splattered with crises. It seems that time *runs out* on some realities. Some relationships sour and end. Jobs often disappear. Careers lose their allure. Bodies break down. Parents become ill and die. Nerves fray.

Many men, at this period, lose their *will to be* and sink into depression or slide into addictive behaviour. Alcohol, sex, drugs, consumerism, religion or multiple relations distract them from the pain of the reality that mid-life offers. In my experience, women are more inclined to face the music and decide to dance — sometimes out of relationships that don't fulfill. Women at this stage of life often will begin a path of self development and strong individuation.

In order to grow forward, *positioning* is important. We choose to live or die within the context of our many deaths at this period. We even choose to live or die in our *final* moments. It is a choice. The choice is about *integration* or *disintegration.*

As our bodies begin a slow slide to the earth where they will eventually rest, we need to choose to strengthen our resolve and our energy towards "coming together" in our spiritual being. The rhythm of the two movements, towards life and death, can bring peace and harmony in our last years. If this is neglected, we simply dissolve into oblivion. I have witnessed many people who had debilitating disease, opt for a trusting future rather than despair. They have died as they lived: gracious, loving and wise. Others, alas, have died "dead," because they chose to live that way.

For Peter, a retired police officer, this last time was anything but a gift in its initial phase. I remember him saying this to me, in a state of utter confusion and despair:

> I've worked since I was fifteen. I've never known anything other than work. Then the chief hauled me in and announced that I was to retire. God, I hate that word! I don't know how to do nothing and just sit around. I miss my buddies on the force. I miss the excitement of the job. I miss the regularity of my life. I want to just kill myself because I don't know how to be here.

After a period of dark desperation, Peter began to enjoy his newfound freedom and, with the help of some good retired colleagues and some support from me — and the patience of a good wife — he managed to grow into peace. He began to devote his energy to helping kids in after-school programs and grew somewhere he had never imagined.

I had asked my friend Marilyn to tell me about her days. Here is what she said in a letter to me. She had taken on the role of state coordinator of *Rainbows,* a program for kids in grief and kids coming from divorced families.

> All in all it's a very full and satisfying life. The fatigue is only part of it. It lets us know

> we are living our lives. I really wanted to write something to you about aging, since I am seventy-one now, but I haven't had time.

Finally, Harold, a man who had been a banker from the age of seventeen, wrote this to me after a seminar I presented to his Rotary Club:

> This is the best time of my life. At last I have time to read those books that I've been buying all those years. I have the time to read about how I should have raised my children, planted my plants and planned my career. You know, I didn't do too badly considering that I "winged it" on my own. I guess that's what I'll have to do for the next years, as well. I trust my instincts as I always have. I had good models for it. My mom lived to be a hundred. Dad died young at eighty-seven.

You have heard as many stories as I have, about lives lived. Toronto's *Globe and Mail* has devoted a section of the back page of the daily newspaper to stories such as these. Lives have been *lived,* rather than *put up with* and there are lots of models all around us for how we might position our last gift of time. Imaginative lives are not limited to the terribly gifted. Imaginative lives are as much the gifts of the extremely poor and uneducated as they are for the rich and famous.

This one's for you!

Beginnings

The gift of waking up is the beginning of wisdom, and wisdom begins just with that — nothing more convoluted, nothing more profound. Waking up. The first moments of each day are the training ground for every moment that follows. In these primary moments the stage is set for the day. Will I be angry? Will I be positive? Will I be cranky? Will I be isolationist? Will I be ... ? This is a capital time for decision making — even if you have awakened tired. Smile or frown. Decide. We can take this primary energy that can begin each day and use it as a springboard for the rest of our lives.

Primary moments are vitally important. Marion Woodman, a Toronto psychiatrist, says that our whole life is shaped by the dynamic of how we were born: natural, Caesarean, premature, breech. So it is, I believe, with each day. The day will unfold as we have positioned ourselves in the first moments. We decide either for hope or for despair. Even in the sadness of being sick, being bereaved, being imprisoned, we have choices to make for or against life. We can choose to live with *imagination* or choose the prison of hopelessness and rebellion.

From his prison cell in 1897, Oscar Wilde wrote: "… he who is in a state of rebellion cannot receive grace … "

Negative energy blocks the gifts that life can bring. It destroys the inner harmony that we are born with and that we experience time and time again in our lives. But some are wont to apply brakes to their graceful growth and stubbornly refuse to allow positive energy into their being. They become stuck in a quagmire of despair and disallow any generosity of spirit to break through. Some even gloat in that negative state and mirror the Scrooge of Dickens' fame. They dismiss their own imagination and certainly the imagination of anyone else.

Wilde was intrigued by the author, H.K. Huysmans, who said that imagination transcends the vulgar reality of existence. The true artist of life is able to see in the ordinary, extraordinary opportunities for life and beauty.

Imagination is that primary power within us that enables us to cast a spell on each moment. It encourages us to take the flesh of life rather than the ashes of death. I have known people who live in a state of constant depression, rage and rebellion, not because of a sad episode but because they have become addicted to grief, and after a while, have chosen to stay there in an intoxicated manner. To live within the realm of imagination, on the other hand, is to delve into the imaginable with the transforming muses of the unimaginable, even in the simplest of things.

Creative living allows for mistakes. Life becomes an art when we choose which moments are capital for our future. Mistakes are always part of the kaleidoscope of our days and nights. In the reality of visual art, it is often the things that were initially mistakes that end up hanging on museum walls. Perhaps they reflect the moments that were dared, and out of the *daring*, imagination, creativity, and entirely unimagined energy and opportunities emerged.

You have to trust your potential for imagination. Otherwise, you're unlikely to ever start to venture into new territory. And this is a time of your life for new territory, if you desire to venture forth.

When I was a young man, we used to tease about the inexhaustible icon, Charles de Gaulle, who had an utter trust in himself. We told a story that he would rise every morning with a smile on his face and look at the statue of the Sacred Heart of Jesus and proclaim, *"Sacré Coeur de Jésus, ayez confiance en moi!"* (Sacred Heart of Jesus, trust in me!).

His juxtaposing the traditional ejaculatory prayer was sacrilegious, I thought. But the longer I live, the more I think he was not out of line. Creator, trust that I am a good, exciting, venerable, creative and eternal being. Trust that!

New language

I awoke, a while back, to the fact that I am no longer *fifty-something*. I had never imagined *sixty*. It didn't feel any different from thirty. I didn't look that much different from pictures of myself in my forties, and fifty was just yesterday. But sixty didn't make much sense. I have talked to some of my elders about being old and most of them have told me that they didn't feel old until quite a bit later. They eventually moved from *feeling old* to *being old.* I know I am involved in this dance of aging, but I don't feel it most of the time. I know that it is happening to me, and I cannot stop the music.

Yesterday, I used to think about the future as though there was a surplus of time ahead of me. Now I realize that there are ten or twenty, or perhaps only four or five, years in which to do the things I wish to do before I die. I realize, finally, that time is more than money and that the gift of time I am given each day is truly my last gift of time.

I realize, as well, that many of the things that defined me so well, the things I strove for relentlessly, don't really mean that much to me anymore. They feel like somebody else's script, somebody else's definition of what it means to be valid. I have achieved a level of being, a shade of being, a repertoire of actions that have defined me. As the song from *La Cage aux Folles* says:

> I am what I am. I am my own special creation. So, come take a look, give me the hook or the ovation. It's my song....

♪♪♪

Recently, I watched a TV special called *The Great Canadian Dream* on our national station, CBC. There had been invitations for artists to enter the contest. There was a cash prize available, a TV special in the winner's name and a host of other gifts. It amazed me to find that not one of the finalists was over thirty!

I had spoken to a music publicist earlier in the year to discuss the possibility of sending my newest CD to the major radio stations for airplay. She was very gracious. She has known me for many years. She is almost my age. Then the verdict: "You are too old." My voice doesn't sound old, my hair is gray (what's left of it), my energy is high and I am generally looked upon as a fairly youthful man. But I was too old! Over thirty is old in that industry and over thirty doesn't sell.

The culture we inhabit lives with this script. Now and again I am devastated by this kind of reality.

We are the second generation that is not surprised to live to be very old. There are lots of us living to be over a hundred. The generation that preceded my parents was surprised if they lived beyond fifty. Now we are shocked when someone dies in their fifties or sixties.

My aunts and uncles embraced a state that made them "modern" unto death. They dressed with panache, had opinions on the past and the present and shared their opinions openly. They did not ape their ancestors, but often went quite against the grain. They explored, dared and entered into the future with gusto. Yet, few of them had an expectation that they would grow into and *grow* in old age. They did, however, for the most part, grow old, survived the journey and did what they needed to do in order to maintain dignity and health.

We are the first generation that is in the process of creating a language and syllabus for *elder-growth*. We are designing a new model for aging. Since we have not had an adequate language for the project, we need to create new language in order to be able to shape new ways of *being old* in the future — new ways of *being old* that are not demeaning and derogatory.

That language is as much about a way of being as it is about words to describe our being. We often joke about our age. As some would say, "It is nothing to joke about." In fact, it is something we would be less inclined to joke about if we truly embraced it as a valid and important event. Growing old is a major project and one that could and should take up all the time and energy we have. The less we accept it as an inevitability and rather view it as an opportunity, the more we will be inclined to bother positioning ourselves towards the future, rather than putting on the brakes or treading water.

New horizons

No chapter of our life is a mistake. Each moment of our story contributes to the story. We have had moments in our lives that were so traumatic we didn't think we'd manage to crawl out of them. The challenges, the obstacles, the people involved made life seem unbearable. That was then. Now we can look back on those moments and realize that they were pivotal in defining our future.

At times we could wish they never happened. But they did. At times, we can look back on them with disbelief — that they indeed did happen, or that we survived them. But we did. Scarred, sometimes bitter, relieved, sometimes confused. But alive!

Why not do a fearless inventory of the past and identify some of those pivotal moments? Remember them. Recreate them. Try to feel, once again, the feeling that arose: courage, liberation, elation, challenge, fear, terror, dis-smell, dis-taste, remorse, rage. Whatever it was, feel it. Remember how deeply tremendous the obstacles seemed, how horrible the consequences of your choices, or how liberating the results of your action could be. Your emotional intelligence is not something to disregard. So feel deeply once again what you felt at that moment. That feeling can breed wisdom as much as your reason can. Don't be afraid to grow this way.

What went on? Who were the players? What was *really* going on? What pushed you to a decision? What pushed you over the edge? What made you freeze in fear or charge on with courage? Recreate the scene. You lived through it. It is worth remembering. And better yet, not forgetting …

What were the gifts of that event? Wisdom? The

resolve to always tell the truth? The opportunity to face the future with pride? Dignity? Wounds that had healed? Trust?

Trust in the future is built on experience. Trust grows in us as a result of lessons learned, stories told and lives lived. It is as much a positioning as breathing. We trust because it worked the last time. It is an exercise. After a bout of hypertension when we become breathless, we have to practice trusting that we can breath on our own again. After a heart attack, we have to trust that the heart will beat on its own again — that it will not give out on us. And we have to learn, often for the first time, that we can trust its action.

In a sense, we have to visualize our future over and over again. Otherwise, we can stay stuck, even live in the quagmire of sadness that past battles often implant in our lives. Or we can decide to risk *imagining* a future. That can only be done once we trust that we have survived the past battles.

Start by starting the day right

Will you shower immediately? Dress? Stay in your dressing gown? By this stage of life we generally know ourselves well enough to know what will work. For some, to lollygag in the morning is disastrous — it sets a tone of passivity for the day. For others, it is a respite from years of hurrying. Some find that getting showered, dressed, and fed is the way to optimal living.

Others find that the most beneficial way to start the day is in quiet prayer. For some, it's meditation. For many it is a quiet walk. For others, it is accomplished by walking to the local church or to the temple or synagogue for a communal morning service. Events like this that were impossible in the "working years," now can give the necessary zest to a new day. A time to collect your thoughts, to recollect your life, a time to remember those you love and those you hate. For many who live their lives with heavy grudges or deep, sad memories, this awakening is capital. Some can do it *on their own*. Many prefer to do it *solo*. But for some, a communal gathering feeds their needs. That could take the shape of Tai Chi, coffee at the corner with friends, breakfast with your partner. I know that when I have negative feelings running rampant within me, I have to depend on rituals, parades, crowds and clowns to pull me out of my deaths. Alone, I can easily just *stew*.

Even if you live with another person, it is important to claim some morning time for yourself. Private rituals can help. Time on the toilet. Time sitting by the window or the wood stove with coffee or tea. Time wandering through the garden checking the growth on each plant. Time flipping pages of a magazine, looking at the pictures. Time sitting with some sacred text. Time just sitting looking nowhere, hearing nothing.

It is important to train your partner to your morning patterns. He or she likely got to know you when you were "on the run," trying to get out of the house in the morning to go to work. Now, it is a new person he or she has to meet. You, too, have to meet your own new person, as well as that of your partner. It's like starting a new relationship all over again. In order for this to be successful, it is important to share with your partner what your needs are in the morning. Discover, as well, what his or her needs might be. If they coincide, that's great. If, not, begin the negotiations. It could mean time spent independently early in the day. That does not indicate that you love each other less. It just means that by respecting the other, you might love each other more.

Waking can be a slow process, as well. Some awaken eager to face the day. Some awaken extroverted. Others awaken in a state of cocoon and introversion. We need quiet, gentle movements, quiet, gentle sounds, silence, not the radio. Just slowly coming into our own.

For some, morning awakening stirs up the sexual. There is a need to embrace and to be embraced. Cuddle. Some want sexual intercourse. That has to be negotiated as well, unless you share your life with someone who is on the same wave-length. This time of life could offer you the opportunity, at last, to explore your sexuality and the loving by your partner without kids, rush and obligations. Take time to take the time you need … at long last.

Sometimes we just need to stay in bed. Most mornings can be sculpted to fit what you need. There is no sin in staying in bed for as long as you want. You could sleep (although most of us over fifty find that hard to do after a certain hour), or lie there and think. Read, or have coffee or tea and start the day there. Most of our lives have had early rising prescribed, without tarrying, in order to get out of the house and into the "real world." Chances are, you have realized that it wasn't all that real out there — sometimes more artificial than real — and that a good sleep-in could provide enough energy for almost anything.

Have more pillows than you need, warm blankets and, above all, a comfortable bed. I remember my furniture salesman Uncle Godfrey telling me, when I winced at the cost of a new bed, that we spend more hours in that piece of furniture than in any one place in our day.

Befriend your bed. One day you might have to spend a fair bit of time there. If it has become your enemy, you will not be able to befriend it in old age. Practice now!

I believe we are a generation that has learned to despise early bedtime. To get a few hours of sleep before midnight can give us good energy for the early morning. Certainly, we can turn off the phone or have a service answer it. Our life is not dependent on everyone else's life patterns.

Choose your own way of living.

You might sleep even better without the bad news that the television reports on the evening news. Most likely, your rest could be better without horrible scenes running around in your head. You can live without everyone's pain present in you at all times of the day. We are the first generation to be bombarded with instant tragedy from all corners of the globe. It is not a necessity to listen to or watch the evening news.

I always find that when I am on vacation, I am quite able to live without the bombardment of the media. I find that I don't need daily newspapers. Why not live on weekend editions? Or none at all?

In the same manner, you are not required to wake up to news or music. Bad news can always wait. You don't need noise. You'll still be there to receive it. Perhaps, after a bit of awakening, coffee, tea, breakfast, you might be better suited to deal with it. Why not do your preliminary, positive awakening beforehand?

Most people I know, who have gone "over the hill," have so many things to do that they cannot contain themselves. For others, the prospect of time without end frightens them. For the one group, I say, bravo! But don't forget that older people can burn out and exhaust themselves (and others). Some become whirling dervishes and self-destruct through activism.

Lists are good. They can help some people bring order into chaos. But don't forget that imagination breeds on chaos, as well. From the fermentation in the mind, new ideas can spring. That is always going on whether you program it or not. So why not begin by makings lists? Not just *work lists*, dream lists, trip lists, people lists, book lists.

For the first time in your life, you are likely aware

that there will be an end to your days. Why not choose a number (the higher the better) and think of all the things you'd like to do in those years, people you'd like to see, places you'd like to visit, flowers you'd like to plant, pleasures you would like to experience? You will likely get to some of them. Or, because you have invented your future, you might get to many more because you've *designed* hope.

Some people thrive on regimen. If you are one of them, you might create some sort of daily plan. Rise at a certain time. Pray or meditate. Exercise. Eat breakfast. Shower. Be at your desk at a certain time. Have lunch and dinner at a fixed time. With that in place, you can be happy. Without it, you could find yourself sullen or disoriented.

Others rejoice in the space and time that this period of life gives. Erase the guilt that so often accompanied *doing* in earlier times. Push yourself to let yourself *be* and take all the time that you want for yourself.

Some people live well alone. Others do not. No one has to be completely alone all the time. When I lived alone, at one point of my life, I always tried to invite one friend to share one meal a day with me. I loved that. For some that would be too much. But it gave my extroverted personality the opportunity to share and converse and grow with new people and good old friends. It was a rich, not a lonely, time for me. Some might have that need only periodically. In my experience, it is important to *invite*. Otherwise, people easily forget about you or fear disturbing you.

Even if you live with someone, it is important to create variety in the way you live your day. Have "dates" with your partner. Go to the theatre, church, dinner. Go for walks, read to each other, rent movies. Go out separately with your own particular friends. Some day one of you *will* be alone and you both need to create a network of friends who are also a part of your everyday experience.

Golf, squash, gardening, hiking, book clubs, art courses, choral groups. There are so many ways I see my friends growing somewhere. It is always invigorating for me when I hear that so and so has gone on a trip, run in a marathon, or embraced a new relationship. There is sometimes a new energy that arises with age. Activities that had been forbidden by parents, partners or society can open up brave new worlds.

When I was in Quebec City last summer, I was sitting beside two women my age who had just come out of a book store. We sat on the same bench, overlooking the mighty St. Lawrence River. They had bought travel books about Greece. I could not help but overhear them delighting in the prospect of a trip next year. They carried on about how, when their husbands were alive, they could never have travelled abroad. Their *Shirley Valentine* was awakened and, with their mutual encouragement, they could freely adventure where husbands feared to tread …

As my friend Cornelius said the day his dad died, his mum got on the bus and never got off again …

Book ahead

I have some friends who have lived for years with degenerative diseases. Most of them died as soon as they were diagnosed. They cried, fretted, had their "little funerals," as one friend calls them, and then had to learn to live all over again. Little by little, they discovered that they likely weren't going to die anytime soon and began to reshape their days and nights and their relationships with everything and everybody.

Many of them learned that life had always been as tenuous as it was with this new knowledge that they could die. They just hadn't known it. So they repositioned themselves. So many of these people have become models for the rest of us who live with the illusion that we will live forever. The best lesson I learned from them was that it was best to make plans *anyway.*

Margaret and George went to Europe every few months and enjoyed the home they had created in the south of France. When they learned that the medication George was taking was having a devastating effect on his system, they knew it would ultimately cause his death. But they stuck to their plan. In fact, they booked tickets for the months ahead, months ahead of time. It was a sublime act of trust. It had always worked to that point. Why not the next time?

When they last went to France, the final chapter began to occur. George began to feel ill. He knew that something serious was happening to him. So, they called a taxi to take them to the American Hospital in Paris. George, with his usual flair, exited the hotel with his turtleneck sweater and his linen jacket and proceeded toward the taxi. All the way to the American Hospital, he entertained Margaret with his musings about the architecture, the hedges, the people. It was just another ordinary ride in the *taxi de Paris*. Upon his arrival at the hospital, he suffered a heart attack. During the night, he was found reading the cookbook he had carried with him to the hospital. He so loved to cook! Life was normal. If he was going to die, he was going to die *living*, anyway!

In the few hours that followed, another heart attack occurred and surgery was performed. George died in the process. But George the French professor and musician died as he had lived, with dignity, awareness and trust. And in Paris!

We can decide to live with trust and have an inner contentment, or decide to live with hesitancy and have inner shakiness. I believe we have choices here. I have witnessed so many of my friends choose life and, as a result, they have lived and died with grace while others stubbornly slid into gloom.

2

How to Become Earthy and Grow Up

And if the worldly forget you,
Say to the silent earth,
I flow.
To the swift water say,
I am.

— *Rainer Maria Rilke*

Earth creature

I left the Dominican Monastery after twenty years of life there. My stepfather was furious with me. Living with a world view that put fidelity to the job before fidelity to self, he had a difficult time adjusting to my decision. However, I believe he tried to understand.

In a moment of true compassion, he told my brother to tell me that there was an extra plot in the cemetery in our hometown should I ever need it. That certainly precipitated my thoughts on death — at the early age of forty. How could it not?

Every year or so, I make a point of visiting his grave, alongside my mother's, in that lovely little town where I grew up. The cemetery sits on the outskirts of the town at the end of a road marked *No Exit.* Almost every one of my elders is buried there — from my great, great grandparents to some of my peers. I go there to do some serious reflecting. I listen to the quiet … I look at the sky … I look at the ground … I wonder.

What was once abhorrent to me — to be buried in the ground — is a friendlier prospect now.

The ancient Hebrew story of beginnings calls humans by the name of *adam,* which means *earth creature*. I find it interesting that the most primitive *first story* we have describes this creature as being *of the earth*. That, for me, is our *primary conversion* — to accept that we are just that: creatures of, from and for the earth. Until that conversion is made, we can easily spend all of our lives avoiding the reality of our being. The result is a kind of *pseudo living* — replacing being with having, relationships with things, and pleasure with duty.

The North American First Nations peoples shared the same nomadic wisdom as the Hebrews. Chief Seattle used the following words to address U.S. President Franklin Pierce in 1854:

> How can you buy or sell the sky, the warmth of the land? The idea is strange to us …

> Every part of this earth is sacred to my people. Every shining pine needle, every sandy shore, every mist in the dark woods, every clearing and humming insect is holy in the memory and experience of my people. The sap which courses through the trees carries the memories of the red man...
>
> This shining water that moves in the streams and rivers is not just water but the blood of our ancestors. If we sell you land, you must remember that it is sacred, and you must teach your children that it is sacred, and that each ghostly reflection in the clear water of the lake tells of events and memories in the life of my people. The water's murmur is the voice of my father's father.

Chief Seattle's people had not, as yet, lost the human link with the cosmos. And he continued ...

> The rivers are our brothers, they quench our thirst. The rivers carry our canoes, and feed our children. If we sell you our land, you must remember, and teach your children, that the rivers are our brothers, and yours, and you must henceforth give the rivers the kindness you would give my brother.
>
> The red man has always retreated before the

> advancing white man, as the mist of the mountain runs before the morning sun. But the ashes of our fathers are sacred. Their graves are holy ground, and so these hills, these trees, this portion of earth is consecrated to us. We know that the white man does not understand our ways. One portion of land is the same to him as the next, for he is a stranger who comes in the night and takes from the land whatever he needs. The earth is not his brother, but his enemy, and when he has conquered it, he moves on. He leaves his fathers' graves behind, and he does not care. His fathers' graves and his children's birthright are forgotten. He treats his mother, the earth, and his brother, the sky, as things to be bought, plundered, sold like sheep or bright beads. His appetite will devour the earth and leave behind only a desert.

"He who dies with the most toys, wins!" This has been an epitaph that has haunted the last half of the past century to the point where most of us were raised — very subtly — to embrace it. Most of our lives were spent in the act of accumulation. Some never give it up and so advance into old age still gathering, hoarding and fretting about their survival, either in their own empire or in the *pseudo* empire they often are tempted to bequeath to their children.

One of the sins of the twentieth century has been

defining the self through *having* rather than through *being*. With this vision of reality, success in old age can only come through tangible *things*. How boring this becomes for everyone who has to worship at the shrine of affluence! Seeing the trophies or hearing the tales of someone's past can lead to emptiness if there is no radiance in their stories and positive energy to live on in their legacy. We, as a society, are so apt to deny death. That denial makes us easy prey to the *demons* of the day. Ernest Becker, in his insightful book, *The Denial of Death*, says that when they find our remains in some future time, " … they will think we were nomads, *a people who spent their lives wandering from one shopping plaza to another.*" We can so easily fall into the trap of allowing possessions to define our being and give us value.

Perhaps it is out of a sense of worthlessness or of failed-being, that we shop and acquire in order to validate ourselves. In that sense, we feel that we only have value from some *external referent* rather than from the fact and, indeed, the gift of our being. The North American socio-economic system in which we exist depends almost entirely on this wounded sense of being human. We joke about *shopping till we drop* but most of us have dropped long before we went shopping. In fact, that very system is the source of our need to embellish our being with *things*.

In our civilization the recovery of self is much more complex than the recovery or the uncovering of our story, and its components. It involves, at a very deep level, the absolutely simple reality of discovering our communion with the earth, first of all, and then and perhaps through that, with the entire universe. Let's start with the most obvious and fly to the sublime.

Our property, Ash Croft, comprises twenty-five acres of land that is now in Phase Four of its human history (at least, as our local historians tell it). Early human history tells us that when the First Nations peoples lived here, the land was filled with white pine, oak, hemlock, ash and maple.

With the arrival of the British, the trees came down and the farming phase began. The lumber was sent to England to be used for furniture and shipbuilding. It took about one hundred years to destroy what had been an earthly paradise. Farming on this rocky, sandy, heavily forested land frustrated the settlers.

In the nineteen-sixties, when the land became arid and was no longer arable, the government urged farmers and landowners to reforest and a new phase was begun. Thousands of white and red pine, maple, black walnut, red oak and ash trees were planted.

Now the trees have grown, after thirty-five or so years. The land has been refreshed with years of decaying vegetation and a new phase has begun. Once again mushrooms abound, nuts cover the earth, sumac with the brightest red plumes and old apple trees produce wonderful fruit for the deer, rabbits, squirrels, wild turkey and every sort of life. These are all creatures that were forced to flee for survival before the murderous hands of the Europeans who stole the continent from the native tribes, as well as from animals and birds. Now the fields are once again filled with the ancient flowers that had gone into hiding as the marauding Europeans cut down the trees and destroyed the flora.

The dance continues as urban sprawl attempts to eat up the land. The future life will require sensitive and informed decisions regarding the health of the environment for all the inhabitants of this neighbourhood.

Along with the reforestation projects that our government had the wisdom to introduce, we need to have a reforestation program *for our human lives*.

In the three generations or so that have taken us away from the land, we have jeopardized our "human" or "humus" lives. We have lived with the illusion that concrete and *un-messiness* are our birthright. On the contrary, earthiness and messiness are essential elements for the soup that makes up human living.

The first conversion we should attend to, in the twenty-first century, is to our earthly identity. For the sake of the earth, and for the sake of our ability to live *and* die we must become more "earthly-minded."

In my education — both at home, at school and, indeed at church, I was encouraged to be more "heavenly-minded." I know now that it was an unwise notion to plant in the mind of a city boy. By virtue of the fact that I was concrete-bound in the city, I would anchor myself in the streets rather than the fields. My body and soul were *out of harmony* with nature.

My ancestors, who left Europe to come here and farm, lived within another geography. I hardly knew their geography — even though I was raised a short distance from where they homesteaded upon their arrival in Canada. The religious imperative to fly above nature, which was the legacy of my faith tradition, led me to a dangerous zone for a human. I moved into *mind and spirit* and shifted out of the fundamental arena for a human — namely, the earth. I was trained to disregard our dwelling place.

I try to look back at my own genesis as a human. I was conscious, at an early age, of my relationship to the world around me. Yet my first memories seem to centre on being part of the people around me. Photographs capture people in my story. Tales are told that remind me of my ancestral roots (at least from the mid 1800s). Furnishings ground me in my Alsatian-Irish-Ontario beginnings. But there is little on my palette that reminds me of my truest earthly roots.

When did I become conscious of being "of the earth?" Was it at the funerals when grandparents were laid to rest in the ground at the cemetery? They were buried there after having been waked in the living room for three days, while we ate dinner in their presence in the dining room. Was there a link between this life and the earth? Perhaps.

Was it at the burial of a dead bird discovered in the yard? Or a butterfly that we pinned to a piece of velvet? Or, saddest yet, the death of Skippy, my dog?

I had heard that Mum lost a baby, (in fact, six), but

they seemed to disappear as if they were only a concept. I never saw them. Death created sadness in the house but I don't believe it ever really *grounded* me.

It was, on the other hand, the wondering at the skies, the movement of the clouds, the falling of the rain and snow that created an awareness in me that there was more to me than what I saw. However, it was an upward awareness and tended to pull me into the ethereal and the religious. Even the "holy cards" the nuns gave us, or the memorial cards that commemorated our departed, were wont to have clouds, skies, sunrises or sunsets on them. Perhaps it was to help us forget our humble, yet glorious *human* nature.

It was in the consciousness of my own inevitable death, that my re-grounding took place. It was not so much the fact that I would die, but rather the fact that *I* would be buried in the earth. There was a need in me to begin a process of befriending this resting place.

We live with a narcissistic notion that each of us is the only thing that is of importance in the world. Since the time of Descartes, we have each become the centre of the universe. We have lost the sense of *link*. Link to the universe, to the earth, to the community, to history. That is likely the root of our selfishness, our materialism and our injustices. Having alienated ourselves from the rest of the ecosystem, we centre on our own needs and desires. We have become *ego-centric* rather than *eco-centric*. And more and more we are becoming aware that there is no health in that — either for ourselves or for the universe.

The spirituality that reigned, from the Reformation onwards — both in Catholicism and in Protestantism in the Christian tradition — insults our earthly nature. It casts a shadow of suspicion over our humanity and positions it as a result of a terrible primordial *fall* rather than granting it the right to be our primary *blessing*. It is because of this attitude, I believe, that we are living in a soup of ecological and social disaster in this early part of the twenty-first century. We continue to live as though we were not *of the earth*. And with the terror of religious fundamentalism that reigns in our epoch, fueled by fear and rage, we will have a hard time balancing an act that will prevent the annihilation of the earth and its beauty.

Our personal *recovery* is where we can start. Little by little we can re-root ourselves in the earth and live with the dignity of earth creatures who come from the elements of the earth and who return there in death.

I attempt to do this in a variety of ways. It is, perhaps, at this age that I am able and am interested in this great discovery of my true being. Perhaps it has always been so. In my memory, older people seemed to be much more interested in the earth. Now that I am growing older, this is the time for me to recover that essential aspect of my being.

How can you make this happen in your own life?

Down to Earth

We are, by our very nature, creatures of the earth. It is

easy for us to forget it. Ernest Becker says that we are "gods who shit." It is easy to get caught up in the "gods" part and forget the other part of the equation.

I can remember the joy I experienced when I once had a condominium overlooking Lake Ontario. I thought it was the most delightful prospect — to be able to look at the lake day and night. It took me a few weeks to get over it. After that point, I was surprised at how grey it was most of the time. Little by little it became wallpaper for me. I was more annoyed at the spiders and the pigeons that gathered on the balcony than overjoyed that I could wonder at the waves.

This is always a hazard: to be unaware of where we are *planted.*

I am constantly amazed at how there has been a rebirth of two movements in the past few years: gardening and spirituality. This is not at all surprising when you recognize that the two are fundamentally linked — most especially since those approaching middle age find it necessary to do a reality check after the cosmetics of pretending have turned to powder.

Possibly you have a small patch of garden. Or maybe you have a few pots and some soil on your balcony. *Get into it!* Feel it, smell it, get your fingers and toes into it!

This is a way of conversion for those of us who were bred to disdain dirt. Fewer and fewer of us were raised on the land. Unlike our ancestors before us, many of our contemporaries were raised on concrete or in the air, in apartments. Earth, stones, bugs and worms are all foreign to our daily experience. As a result, we are inclined to disregard them. They have become wallpaper to us.

Most of our cities and towns have woods in and around them. Forests are places of human longing and comfort. If they are not found on the outskirts of the town or city, often they are created through parks in the interior spaces. As humans, we seem to need places within which we can sequester ourselves. We depend on them for food, wood, safety and silence.

It is not at all surprising that Dante speaks of the mid-life clarification taking place in the middle of a wood:

Nel mezzo del cammin di nostra vita
mi ritrovai per una selva oscura
che la diritta via era smaritta.

In the middle of the road of my life
I awoke in a dark wood
where the true way was wholly lost.

— *Dante Alighieri*

Woods create a womb for us in the midst of the maelstrom of life. They are dark, moist, verdant places where we are invited to reflect. They become a palette for adventure. The sombreness of the forest offers us the womb for interiority. The interconnectedness of everything that grows there can trigger our imagination about our own place on this earth.

Reflect on how everything supports everything else. Rotting vegetation creates the womb for new growth. Diversity exists side by side and creates the harmony of the forest. Moisture is stored there for the days of drought. Food and habitation are made available for all who live there. Though it is self-contained, it is linked to and supports the world in which we live.

Its breathtaking beauty urges us to admire. Its *chiaroscuro* creates the mood for reflection. Its soft underpad, created from centuries of droppings, creates the stage for future development. It truly is the gauge of the ages. We ought to go there often.

Another spot to pitch your tent is at your family or community cemetery. It helps bring everything into focus. It is not a place for answers, but is, indeed, a place that prompts questions. Why am I here? Where will I be after this? What is the significance of my life? Of everybody else's life buried here? What about the people and things that capture me now? Where do they fit into the picture? Are they worth the energy or investment? What time is it on *my* journey?

In the last century, most people were buried in the community cemetery that was, if not beside the churches where the people gathered regularly, at least within the town limits.

In most European communities, people were buried, allowed to decompose and then their bones were cleaned off and put into a box to be stored in a mausoleum. This was done by family members. Little by little, one was educated to the reality of death. Everyone was involved. The "earth-creature-liness" was clear.

With the *pornographication* of death in our generation, we drift farther and farther from our roots. I believe that if we were more aware of the end, we would do better at living the in-between. I am not talking about eternal salvation, or anything as haughty as that. We need to become comfortable living the here and now as a *part of* the earth rather than *above and beyond* and *despite* it! Only then will we be able to comfortably grow into our death.

One of the most stunning humans I have ever met was an old woman, Mrs. Midlaer. She was a woman who immigrated to Canada from Holland. She had spent some of her years in a concentration camp in Indonesia during World War II. In that arid and hostile environment, she planted a few seeds that grew into plants and produced flowers. She used to tell me about the hope that the process of the growth of seeds to plants gave her in her life. In the midst of desperation and terror, these plants beckoned her and her comrades forward. They lived in her mind and heart all her life and still live in mine.

I met her when she was in her nineties. She used to come to our monastery every day and spent hours watering the *impatiens* in the cloister walk. These were plants that were outside all summer. She would bring them in before the frost hit and would keep them alive all winter. Every day she would come to visit them and with a small metal instrument, blow mist on their leaves. And with such care! She sang to them and spoke to them, sharing with them and us her lovely energy. Her grace transformed everyone who met her. Her grace transformed all of us, as well, who walked by her lovely flowers.

Every year I tend my perennial gardens. Most of the plants in my garden came from friends. I can walk among the plants and link them to the people in my life. I have had to get to know them. Some, which should have been planted at the back, were too tall to be in front. But that's where I put them before I knew them. Some are biennial and disappear after two years. Some don't like to be disturbed. Some are sensitive to sun or shade. Others require certain soil conditions. Some have disappeared, never to return. Others grow where they weren't planted. Some overtake everything around them. Some need space, air.

They are a gift for me. In order to assure their well-being, I was introduced to a new element: compost. It has become a source of deep spirituality for me. Now, all the scraps from our kitchen go into the composter. What was once a beautiful fruit has nourished us and then what remains has decomposed and become a life-source for something else. One thing gives life to another.

Another element of gardening that re-roots me is the fact that I must touch and be touched by the earth. I become one with it as I work it. It *works at me* while I *work it*. It is a very mysterious synergy that develops and one that could help me recover soul for my journey.

If I have lost my identity as an earth creature, I have lost my soul. But I can recover it. These are a few of the ways. I believe this is more fundamental for our civilization — especially in the First World — than spiritual recovery. It is through this one way that we will be able to grow other aspects of our life — living and dying.

Silence

It is in the stillness that we attend to our truest being. In the din of noise that surrounds us on a constant basis in our present world, we are distracted from the sound of our own heartbeat as well as the sound of the heartbeat of the universe. It is only in the silence that we are able to integrate with our own ecosystem.

I am always astounded when I sit with any of our friends' animals, to see them busy with the world around them. They hear, smell and see things that I am unconscious of. They are forever going after something or other. Their gaze is often glued to an object that is invisible to me until it happens to move. Then, off they go.

I know that I have the same abilities but they have been dulled. They have been silenced by my body's heaviness, by the clutter in my mind and the unwanted sounds that break the wonder of the silence.

Now and again I awaken in the night and venture

out of doors to listen. Pure silence. Then I begin to undress my mind of the heavy cloak that keeps my being from uniting with the sounds of silence that envelop me. Only then can I begin to hear the messages and the voices of the universe that are essential to my mental and spiritual health — and maybe my physical health — as well. The silence of the night allows me to access the deepest parts of my being. The questions arise that will lead me to peace. And often, the responses come to me that I would never have imagined. New solutions to troubles. New directions for dilemmas. New hope in despair. Often the sounds of the universe, the utter silence of the creation can bring me to the unity and peace that is so desired.

I know that if I fail to find silence, I become distracted from my being and enter into the muddle of life. I miss that essential part of my being where integration happens.

Groups of people often come to Ash Croft for retreats. The greatest gift we can give them — especially city folk — is the opportunity to go for a walk through the property. I used to begin each session with a talk. But, little by little, I began to realize that what the people needed when they came here was not more information. Certainly, that is part of the experience and an important one, but not likely the most important reason for them to be here.

It was with a group of community care nurses who wanted a session on burnout that I realized that the best gift I could give them was silence and the opportunity to taste it. The first group I took on a silent walk on the land was overwhelmed with the experience of the quiet. They yearned for it, but had forgotten how important it could be for them.

The practice of silence can be a pivotal school for old age. As we enter into a state of *contemplativity*, as our systems begin to shut down, fear can be overwhelming. The serenity that silence begets is a jewel in the human crown. Without *practice*, this state, which is essential to our nature, is almost impossible for the contemporary human. We are so overcome with noise that constant vibration is considered normal to us. Peace and quiet are so easily attainable but, like any new experience, need to be accessed. And that takes practice.

Why not begin now? Put down this book and enter into a silent state. Close your eyes, or focus on some item in the space you find yourself. Take time. Sit comfortably, or walk. Don't be bothered with tasks for a few minutes. Settle into the silence … silence … silence …

Make a date with yourself to rise in the night and sense the quiet. Or rise early in the morning. Find a time daily when you can linger and listen to the sounds of silence. No music. Nothing but you and the quiet. In your room. In a park. Just you.

Take time periodically, to spend a day by yourself, without other human company. Your pet might accompany you, since animals live in silence and might teach you that life can be beautiful without the clamour of the days and nights that we experience.

Little by little, the sounds that infiltrate will disappear and become white noise. You will attain a new state of being that you will likely enjoy. But it is essential to give yourself the opportunity to experience it.

You might even encourage your closest friends, even your spouse, to enjoy that kind of quiet time with you. Sitting or walking.

When I lived in the Dominican community, there were sometimes periods of tension. Now and again, instead of praying with words, or having meetings to resolve conflicts, we would sit in silence. There was often more healing in intentional silence than in words and actions.

There was also an old saying in the Order that *silence is the father of the preacher.* It is in the stillness and the listening that fresh ideas often emerge. Any writer knows that the imagination works overtime in the silence. It is in my daily walks that insights arise, that conflicts are resolved and some of the most delightful internal experiences take place.

And it doesn't cost a cent.

Sickness

Much of my work is done with hospital staffs throughout North America. As a result, I get to meet with thousands of medical professionals. Their main work is likely thought of as getting people better again. In many cases, that happens. People come for their stay at the hospital, get better and return home. Many don't have such luck and have to face major crises about life and death or, harder still, life and dying. Sometimes what started out as a check-up ends up being a major time of life-assessment.

The image that seems to imprint itself in my mind about sickness is that of the desert. It invites us into a space we fear. Hospitals are seldom places of radical joy. Generally they are arenas for our in-between, transitional times. It is there that we are often *forced* into reflecting on the meaning of our existence and the role of relationship in our life. Desert is an arid space initially. Distractions seem to be absent at first. However, in the solitude and *dépuiment* (unclutteredness), soon the demons appear. When we are stripped of our external covers, we are invited, perhaps even forced, into facing our deepest truths. There are only a few things that matter. What matters?

The gift of this isolation is a preparation for the kind of *face-to-face* reality that most of the mystical traditions describe as happening to us in death. I have seen marvellous manifestations of deep humanity and compassion flow from people who have spent time in the desert of suffering. So many have become delightfully human in the last months of life once they recollected themselves in one spot and put their life in its truest context — that of having an end.

It is also a privileged time for learning the art of *letting go.* We generally take most aspects of human reality for granted. Suddenly, there is an overpowering sense that we are not in charge of everything. To stay in control mode is to live in deep sadness. Illness invites us into the practice of *not being in control* and thus we can allow growth to happen. Illness generally comes upon us and tells us something about our lives, our rhythms, our relationships, our work or play. Illness is a privileged time for listening to *every aspect* of our being. Most of the time it takes some gigantic crash for us to be willing to take the time needed to get back into balance.

It is also a time for those around us to appreciate our value. They can spend time with us, have our undivided attention, say things they have never had the opportunity or courage to say before and hear some things from us that might affect all of our lives. It is also a school for all involved, in which to learn that life might not always be as it was, that the patient might not be here for long. It is a vital time for figuring out whatever needs to be figured out.

It is also an important time of life to listen to the body. Are your *chakras* integrated? Is there distress in one or another of them that prevents you from enjoying good health? Pay attention to your aches and pains.

Listen to your inner rumblings and grumblings. You can enjoy your body late into life if you learn to pay attention to what your body tells you.

My old mentor, Gerry Judd, once told me when I was in my forties that I had a most radiant face. He spoke to me of my *chakras*, those aspects of my human energy that manifest in the various regions of my body system. My upper *chakras* were marvellous. But my lower *chakras*, associated with emotions, sexuality, as well as the base *chakra* associated with grounding and survival, were flaccid. I had spent most of my life subduing, or at least trying to subdue, my fundamental human and therefore divine energies. In attempting to be more God-like, I gave in to a tradition that failed to understand that integration of all the *chakras* could bring about sanctification.

In my experience, many people who deny the lower *chakras* develop into sad and self-indulgent old people. Not all, but many.

What areas of your system are crying out for attention? What things do you have to work on in this final phase of your human life in order to become full, content and holy? Can you do it alone, or would you benefit from the assistance of a coach, a trainer, a guru, a doctor or a therapist? The secret to true growth is honest listening — listening with *all* the senses.

Little illnesses, like the flu or the common cold, can present great opportunities for growth. Most people don't want us to be around them when we are ill. Actually, we don't generally feel much like being around anyone either. But, if old scripts still dominate, chances are that we will force ourselves to "work." However, these times could be perfectly honourable times for peace, quiet and reflection. They are terrific "little schools" for the big illnesses that have greater things to teach us. To deny the energy of illness is to deny the energy of good growth. So, the next time you are afflicted with a cold, an injury, a migraine, try to honour it. Cocoon. Just hide for a while.

Your illness can also be an opportunity for those who care for you to grow with you. Give them the opportunity to exercise kindness and charity. Allow them the opportunity for compassion. Many people will blossom when they have the chance to visit, to cook, to clean your house for you. Don't deprive them of that chance. They can grow as well. Your illness can give them a chance to reflect on their own health and on the deep meaning of mutual existence. I have seen many closed, frightened people become stellar when their partner or friend has truly needed them. We are all good people. Often we just need the chance to shine.

Pets

Pets ground us.

Some learning happened in school. Most learning happens at home — if we pay attention. The introduction of a pet into a household is often the best gift we can receive. I have often thought that we are given pets so we can become human.

Never did I so deeply understand this as when our beloved Morgan died. He was only five. Tears run down my face as I write about him, for he was indeed the best friend this man could ever have had. His presence with us for those few years was a great instructor in life. Besides making us laugh more often than we are wont to, he made us wonder at life. To sit and wonder with him, quietly — *simply sit* — was an absolute lesson in contemplation. On the other hand, to throw the ball, chase after squirrels, roll over on the floor with him and dance together to whatever music was on the radio, swim with him and fetch sticks in the water was a blessing. It allowed our inner child to come out of a deep chill that living life in the modern world can sometimes inflict upon us.

He would comfort us in our illness, troubles, fears and sorrows. Greet us in the morning with a bound upon the bed at 6am. Lead us into our own deaths as we placed his still warm body into the ground near the creek in what we call our *sanctuary.*

Every kind of pet seems to enter into a different chasm of our being. They lead us to wonder, to play, to adventure. They teach us to stretch, to face realities we avoid without them, and they comfort us in our sorrow. They make the earth-bound aspect of our being both respectable and accessible. They also bring us closer to the earthly realities that we are prone to avoid in our sterile and sterilized world.

Pets play the role of the visible thread that runs throughout our lives. In many homes, they *settle* the home because they are the ones most frequently there. They sometimes provide the common language when all other language fails. They command attention and have the ability to pull us out of slumps. Companionship is their best gift. They accompany us through most of our human activities. How difficult it was to go shopping after Morgan's death. How empty the car felt. He had been there at every critical event. He consoled me when I was ill. He was my confessor and confidant. He was my pal and faithful playmate — and all without condition (although a doggy treat could help now and again!).

The experience of witnessing your pet's dying is a great gift, but oh so difficult. The care, compassion and attention that a pet's final illness stirs up in us is immense. They lead us to wonder, to ponder, to attempt to figure out what disease, life and death are all about. In fact, pets teach us how to die.

Morgan died from lymphoma cancer. In the weeks just before his death, he would go off on his own, sit in the woods and look upwards. We would see him sitting there in a contemplative state. Or he would just quietly lie beside the house. Even squirrels didn't grab his attention. It was as though he was intent on dying. It was serious business. Now and again he would look at us with sad eyes and tell us that he was going. Or he would look at us in the middle of the night when he would have to go out and tell us that he needed us to help him *go*. It was so sad but so valuable for our growth. As he had often taught us how to live, he was now teaching us how to die.

Our veterinarian friend Dave came to "release his soul." We held him as he received the injection and we felt him leave us. We all cried and held on to each other tightly. He had become our family. Even our vet's.

Then we carried him down to a spot by the creek, which he had chosen (we believe).We wrapped him in his yellow towels and lay him into the earth. It was normal. It was good and right. It was what is supposed to happen to us, I believe. We covered his body with earth and tears and put our beloved Morgan to rest. He had done his work.

He had created humans and dignified their living and dying … by his.

I always thought that a cat was just a cat. Until I lived with a few. So many people are able to have cats because they are adaptable, independent and need so little care. And they fit easily into almost anyone's lifestyle.

Cats are able to cuddle into us as no other being can. Their warmth can infuse any body with comfort. Their purring can be a great source of consolation and peace. They are very effective in pulling down our blood pressure — although now and again, they manage to raise it a bit with their antics. Cats generally live longer than many animals and can be good friends as we grow through many of our difficult times at a variety of stages of our life.

Whatever pet you choose to be your household companion, it will invite you to stretch. Household pets can lead you to delight and to despair. They also keep you growing. Many times they prime you for your attitudes regarding other humans.

Roots

I am always taken aback when I walk through the streets of Rome, to see a civilization unearthed beneath my level of existence. It makes me aware that I am built on top of those people and their world, as the oak is built on the aspen and the pine that predated it and nurtured the soil that would allow it to blossom at this time of history. I am made aware of the fact that I am not alone. I am linked to everything and everyone that has been and as a result am linked to everyone and everything that will be.

> We are stardust; we are golden; and we've got to get ourselves back to the garden.
>
> — *Woodstock, 1968.*

We can choose to live in isolation on the edge of a small planet, or to live deeply within it.

Who we are and where we came from is a journey that beckons. We can access so much of that information by visiting the wonderful museums that have been built in all our towns and cities. Visiting the British Museum, the City of London Museum, The Museum of Civilization in Gatineau, the Louvre, the Getty, the Royal Ontario Museum, I am confronted with my human roots. These visits help me situate myself and us as part of a long lineage of humanity that has shaped me and my contemporaries.

Our own local Dufferin County Museum is a masterpiece. It helps me understand the area I am presently planted in — from the topography and the ecology and through the stages of human communities that have inhabited this region.

I can also access my roots on the Internet. Genealogical sources have made it an adventure for me to journey from my desk in my study. I don't even have to leave town!

We can remain small and closed. Or we can expand in so many ways to become aware of how we have grown to where we are and where we could be going. We cannot afford to remain tribal in the twenty-first century.

I was raised as an Anglo-Saxon male. The land I live in now hardly reflects the one I was raised in. We were white, European and Christian. That is no longer the case. I could stay stuck in an old pattern or embrace the new cultures that make up my present world. History, archaeology, art, music, food, dance and worship can all contribute to my personal wealth. I can explore endlessly the culture of the world that supports my life now and grow to be wise, compassionate and open. Or

I can close the door to adventure and remain small and scared.

City and local festivals can open doors for us. The taste of different foods, the smells and sounds that surround dance and ritual, the colours and the languages mingle with the laughter and conversation that humans produce. We can always expand our horizons and become part of a bigger world than the one we knew.

When visiting Niagara Falls a few months ago with some Irish friends, I encountered a busload of Hindu monks. I approached a layman who was travelling with them and asked him about them. He told me that they were a community of monks who had come from India to help celebrate the opening of a new temple, not far from where I live, just north of Toronto. Then he said, "Please, come and join us. We expect about 45,000 guests and would love you to get to know us. Please come."

The colours of our world are here for our tasting. Taste and see how good.

Compassion

In 1979 I was on a spiritual path that would lead me out of the Order I so dearly loved, and into a life I had never dreamed would be mine. I learned that I could never predetermine how or where I would end up. There would always be surprises.

I had gone from Florence, where I was living at the

time, to Zagreb, to meet a *confrère* in the Order who was going to show me the sights of his city and spend some quality time with me. He had just been elected Prior of the Croatian Dominicans.

When I arrived in the monastery of Zagreb — where no one spoke a language I knew — I found that the Prior would be busy in meetings for the days that he had invited me to be there. In fact, he was not even in town when I arrived. I felt desperately lonely and angry.

Upon his arrival, he assigned a brother who spoke a bit of French, to escort me about town. That did not calm my storm. However, we did stop in the one book-store in town that had one shelf of English books.

It was there that I befriended Nikos Kazantzakis, the Crete native who would transform my broken heart into that of an adventurous warrior. It was his description of an encounter with an old woman that gave me solace and pulled me out of my slump.

> I was surrounded by olive groves and vineyards. The vintage still had not begun; the grapes drooped heavily and touched the soil. The air smelled of fig leaves. A little old lady came along. She halted. Lifting the two or three fig leaves which covered the basket she carried on her arm, she picked out two figs and presented them to me. "Do you know me, old lady?" I asked. She glanced at me in amazement. "No, my boy. Do I have to know

you to give you something? You're a human being, aren't you? So am I. Isn't that enough?"

— *Nikos Kazantzakis, Report to Greco*

The story of this human's journey — Kazantzakis — was a most welcome companion to me for the rest of my trip, and still is for this part of the trip. He became my friend. His search for meaning echoed mine. I resonated with his faith and his doubts, his sexuality and his sensuality. His anger and his despair danced with mine and took me into a tango with angels and demons and gave me spirit enough to enjoy them both.

As I have said before, I was raised as a white Anglo Saxon (Celtic) male. The unspoken premise was that we were better than anyone else. That was obvious from our visible success. We lived in Canada. We had it all. We were polite, clean, Christian, educated and free.

My mother had remarried to a man with a WASP name, and I had been adopted by him. I was assured that Walker was the better name to have. Even though we were Catholic, the name was Protestant. I'd have a better chance with it than with my biological father's Alsatian name, *Schuett*. I went to "good" schools and was raised right (*façade* is better than truth).

Fortunately, I was confronted with other cultures before it was too late. The Dominicans offered me the freedom of living in a new culture. At twenty, I became bilingual and embraced both the Quebec culture and the international fraternity of the Order. Colours, languages, history led me to know and understand that we were not better than anyone else — just different — and that others' culture, race and religion had things to offer me and the universe that my narrow little world was unable to embrace or comprehend.

This is where true wisdom develops. The knowledge and experience of the other as other. And yet the deep insight that we are all made of the same stuff.

As we age, we have choices. Either we decide to be open and embrace the universe, or we become closed and centre our life on ourselves.

I propose compassionate living as a model for growth. Thomas Aquinas, the great, fat and fecund Dominican Friar of the 1200s, says that compassion is that virtue by which *one becomes the other.* This is a great lesson for us to learn early in life. We are all part of everything.

Earth creatures are just fine *here on the earth.* As a child raised in the Roman Catholic tradition, I prayed that we should be freed from this " … exile — mourning and weeping in this valley of tears." That was a dangerous desire for an earth creature. Tears, struggle, death. They are part and parcel of what everything on this earth lives through in order to grow. To live with the illusion that that will change is disastrous. We should not waste our time escaping to other places, other identities, other realms. It is in living *here* that we engage our lives in any hereafter that we might believe awaits us. Not by awaiting a golden time where all is calm, all is bright. Here and now is it!

It takes a great deal of energy to become compassionate in a world where power and religion dominate, where some are considered better, more saved, more valuable than others. It is hard to become compassionate when it is accepted that the earth is ours to dominate and manipulate to our desires. Where concrete supersedes farmland. Where the automobile rules the shape of our lives and our communities. Where the bottom line enslaves human stories. Compassion is a gate to freedom and delight.

The awareness of our final destiny is a great leveller. It is easy to consider oneself above everything and everybody as long as there is no end to earthly life. But as we age, we become more and more aware that one day our story will be in the obituary column of the local newspaper. No one avoids that. But it is generally only in aging that we *know* this to be true *for us.* It is then that the mighty and the small are one and the same.

Andrew Hudgins' poem says it all:

> Quit snivelling! Sit still!' And in disgust
> he palmed my head like a basketball
> and forced it down and buzzed the
> clippers up my neck again.

Half a century later …

But now, it's his turn and he sits,
Hands folded on his lap, unsteady,
While I, with tiny scissors, snip
The gray hair curling from his nostrils
And from both ears; and, Jesus, at sixty
The death hairs really get their growth,
Don't they? The scissors pinch his skin
And he tries to flinch. "Sit still!"
I smart, and I'm so horrified …
I say it one more time. "Sit still!"

— *The Glass Anvil, 1997*

Big heartedness — magnanimity

Practice getting nice. Work at expanding. Get wisdom from stories about being bigger and better. Exercise your generosity.

Nothing on this earth is "mine all mine." No person, no thing, no title or honour, no job. Everything is a gift. We must learn to live within the energy of each gift, enjoying and developing them while also knowing that we might, at any moment, have to let go.

In order to embrace each gift, it is important to be generous with it. No gift is meant to be hoarded but to be shared.

In his 1970 opening day speech at Tanglewood, the famous summer music school in New York State, the talented and generous Leonard Bernstein said:

It's the artists of the world, the feelers and the thinkers, who will ultimately save us, who can articulate, educate, defy, insist, sing and shout the big dreams. Only the artists can turn the "Not-Yet" into reality. All right, how do you do it? Like this: find out what you can do well, uniquely well — that's what studying is for, to find out what you can do particularly well. You. Unique. And then do it for all you're worth. And I don't mean "Do your own thing," in the hip sense. That's passivity, that's dropping out, that's not doing anything. I'm talking about doing, which means (another old-fashioned phrase) serving your community, whether that community is a tiny town or six continents. And there's no time to lose, which makes your position twice as difficult, because you're caught in a paradox. You see, you've got to work fast, but not in a hurry. You've got to be patient, but not passive. You've got to recognize the hope that exists in you, but not let impatience turn it into despair. Does that sound like double-talk? Well, it is, because the paradox exists. And out of this paradox, you have to produce the brilliant synthesis. We'll help you as much as we can — that's why you're here — but it is you who must produce it, with your new atomic minds, your flaming, angry hope, and your secret weapon of art.

This gracious, mystical man, in the piece *Kaddish Symphony*, which he dedicated to the memory of John Fitzgerald Kennedy, just after his assassination in 1963, talks about this dynamic. The narrator addresses God:

> We have both grown older, You and I.
> And now I am not sad and you must not be sad.
> Unfurrow your brow; look tenderly again
> At me, at us, at all these children
> of God here in this sacred house.
> And we shall look tenderly back to You.
>
> O my Father: Lord of Light:
> Beloved Majesty: my Image, my Self!
> We are one, after all, You and I;
> Together we suffer, together exist.
> And forever will recreate each other.
> Recreate, recreate each other!
> Suffer, and recreate each other.
>
> *— Leonard Bernstein, Closing Prayer, Kaddish (Symphony Number 3)*

A first step in truly becoming magnanimous is to be truly grateful. After so many years of living, we have before us a huge plate of blessings. It is a good time to start to take count of the gifts that have been given to each of us. There have been scourges, but they are not possibly greater than the blessings. From the act of breathing to the act of loving, humans are blessed indeed.

Why not reserve a book for a collection of blessings? Do a relentless inventory of your gifts from the beginning of your days until the present. If you live in sadness and in hopelessness, this list will begin to convert you to your own wealth. Sounds, smells, tastes, feelings, relationships, places, knowledge, imagination. They all hold memory of great benefits. Look at that book now and again when you feel that there is no tomorrow, or that all your yesterdays were in vain.

Why not reserve a day a week for some activity that remembers the gifts received? It might take only thirty minutes, but it could charge you up beyond your imagination. It is so easy to enter into darkness. Why not enter into joy? Perhaps you could have a special place of blessings in your home. Ritualize that activity with a candle, music, soft lighting. It could become a practice that saves your life, or gives you the life you deserve. You are a human being, aren't you? There should be joy in that.

You could begin each day with a gesture of thanks — a smile to yourself in the mirror, outstretched arms in an act of gratitude, a walk that focuses on some of the fine things that have happened to you. You could proclaim a blessing for the gift of food, sunshine, rain, snow, children, friends, health. These gestures serve to enlarge our capacity for loving.

At this stage of your life, you are generally in

charge of your time. If you are not, adjust a few things so that you can become master of your time and space. The time and energy that was spent on work, reproducing, nurturing family and self can now take on a new life that is expansive beyond those boundaries.

Leo and Thérèse had raised their family. Everyone was more or less settled. It was time for them to transfer the loving that had been domestic and local into something larger. They had always worked in the hospitality industry. They sought out international help organizations that could use their energy. So, from mid-life until Leo's death, Leo and Thérèse went from one Third World country to another, bringing their skills and dreams to the lives of hundreds. They expanded themselves, as well, through the joy of embracing new cultures and sharing life with people they wouldn't have dreamed existed. They could have stayed at home and brooded. What models they became for their children and grandchildren and for the entire community that lived around them.

I have met many teachers who, after retirement, used their skills and courage to tutor children and adults who need extra help. Some have gone to work as *English as second language* coaches with immigrant men and women who want to integrate better into life in the new land.

I know of several church and synagogue communities that have instituted a "parish nurse" program. Many of the congregations are aging and those members need life support on many levels from the community base. Some retired nurses embrace this activity. In fact, most of the divinity schools in North America are filled with second and third career men and women who want to give of themselves with a newfound freedom. With a focus on full health (salvation) and a great deal of wisdom and experience to share from their long living, they can contribute greatly to others' lives.

Meals on Wheels, baby sitting, hospice, community clubs and church activities are other ways to stretch. It is amazing to me to see the elders in our local community, through their community arts council, open up their lives and resources to help ensure that educational opportunities in the arts are open to the youth of our community — beyond the schools. Many young people get the inspiration to embrace their dreams, having witnessed the arts being lived by their elders in concerts, plays, writing, studio tours and art exhibits. Money is also collected and generated to help the children advance in the arts. Everybody grows.

Whatever your abilities might have been throughout your life, you can always direct them in new ways until you die. Open up your heart and let the sun shine in …

Honour your mistakes

No one is perfect. At least that is what we say. Generally we become self-destructive because we are not perfect. It is interesting that some of the major prophets of our time have been the artists. In his musical adventure, *Into the Woods,* Steven Sondheim wrote a song, *No One Is Alone,* which asks us to:

> Honour your mistakes
> Everybody makes
> One another's terrible mistakes …

Our mistakes are part of the debris upon which we build our future. They are the compost that gives life and flavour to our days ahead. They are the fodder for forgiveness and ultimately compassion — first towards ourselves and then, towards others. Our mistakes can be fuel for self-understanding and for conversation — with ourselves and with others, as well. Our mistakes can be a great reminder that we are not alone.

So often I have been tempted to say, "I really shouldn't have done that," only to realize that it was indeed *that* which led to so many new opportunities for growth, people, places and new ways of embracing the world.

One time, I was complaining to a psychiatrist colleague and bemoaning the fact that I entered the Christian Brothers when I was fifteen. I had talked about how unhappy I was in my family of origin at that time.

His response to me threw me for a loop. He said that I was a crafty young kid and imaginative enough to find a safe and productive way to leave something that I considered toxic. Indeed, there were many positive aspects to the quasi-monastic life that I lived with these very gracious men for three years. They cared a great deal for me and enabled me to embrace my gifts. The spirituality that they ascribed to is far from where I dwell today. Yet they did instill in me a deep devotion to a simple and wise way to approach the divine.

"Remember that you are in the holy presence of God," was the mantra that was recited every half hour in their classes. The brother who was in charge would simply kneel at his desk for a moment and reflect. Nothing wrong with that. It has stuck with me. There was crazy stuff, too, but that didn't stick.

Often we begrudge the relationships we embraced, the marriages, the commitments that have slipped by, the jobs that almost did us in. They were then and this is now. They all served a purpose for all the parties involved in them. We can bemoan the fact that others were involved in our webs. Mistakes? Perhaps. But also steps we had to take along the way.

Sensuality and sex

Sex is, indeed, the lost chord in the process of human integration. It is that vital element of our being that is the core energy of human activity and of human spirituality. It is so sad that both church and society have lived in such terror of this untamable tiger. It is a shame that we were taught to live with sex as an enemy to our goodness. We were made to hate and mistrust that which could, if grown properly, lead us to the divine.

This last period of our life could take us to new heights in our sexual growth. Gone are the days when sex meant pregnancy. Gone are the days when the old constructs, or old phantoms, overwhelm our imaginations. This is a time for integration of all sorts of basic energies.

Claim your body. This is an essential aspect of sexual recovery and discovery that many in our generation need and, indeed, crave for. Most of us — especially if we were raised in an orthodox religious community — were taught to abhor our bodies. Rather than being a playground for the divine, they were considered to be a war-zone. I can remember one client coming to me and asking me what parts of her body her boyfriend was allowed to touch without it being mortal sin. She wanted me, indeed, to take a magic marker and delineate which areas were safe and which were not. I asked her whether she was truly concerned about offending God (strange language) but she assured me that she only wanted to "get away with as much as possible and still avoid the pains of hell."

In writing this, I realize how strong that language was in my youth. *Sexual sin* was never gray — always black or white — indeed, always black! God seemed to be always offended by sex. Always. And the pains of hell awaited anyone who had an "impure thought, deed or action." It is so sad to think that sexuality was mostly looked upon as deviant — never a gift to explore, but a temptation to avoid. It was that attitude that has stifled so many of us.

Post-mid-life is a good time to vacuum out some of the notions that stifled us in our youth — on all levels of our being. It is a valuable time to own our feelings, our information, our judgments, our decisions and our relationships. Our being will always be coloured by our past. But we do not have to be a victim of it. Our sexuality is one area that needs deep cleansing, because it has been posited as such a hostile enemy.

Take time to know and enjoy your body. It is not an enemy unless you make it so. Look at yourself. Touch yourself. Take time with yourself. Explore every centimetre of your flesh and befriend it. You likely have put on weight, become wrinkled and gray. But that is the mature self that you can embrace. Many of us reject the new state of our being and idolize the body of our youth. Yet, for many of us, there is a possibility of having a better, stronger and leaner body in these last years than we had in our youth.

Explore your sexual energy and feelings by yourself. Perhaps you have failed to know yourself and have put your energy into pleasing others in sexual activity. Befriend your own sexual pleasure and rejoice in it. Often later in life sexual energy is more interior and quiet. That can be a lovely gift to be enjoyed. Self love requires immense discipline that requires us to "pay attention" to our being. The alternative is to dry up and be sad.

A very credible and exciting woman in her seventies told me some time ago that she avoids looking at herself in the mirror. She *feels* young inside. It is only when she looks in the mirror that she realizes that she has become an old woman. But that avoidance seems to be a way of avoiding the maturity that could be embraced by dancing with the old body. That old body manifests the old woman to the world and to herself. Gracious, warm, wily, tough and gregarious! What a gift she has been for a long time. And the wrinkles, furrows and tears have all contributed to make true beauty visible to all who dare look deeply. On the surface, old is old. On the inside, old is beautiful. Don't bury that venerable old treasure under a bushel basket. Manifest it! It is grand!

At this stage of your life, you might be in a relationship or you might desire to explore sex with another. Try not to live by old scripts that judge performance and keep scores. There can be new avenues to explore, new energies to embrace and undiscovered nuances to enjoy.

Maybe you don't function in the same ways as you did in your younger days. Or, better yet, maybe you are growing and can function *in new ways* as you mature in your sexual expression — ways that you would never have had the imagination to explore when younger! Or didn't dare! As Billy Joel says, "The good old times weren't always that good and tomorrow ain't as bad as it seems … ." Don't judge your sexual present by your past. There could be chapters you have yet to explore.

Love for your sexual partner can grow in these latter years. There might have been a sprinkling of it in your youth, but love directed at self and at the other is the main elixir for a passionate and full maturity. What began as lust in a long-term relationship can be an entry point to deepening love in the last period of life.

In some cases, deep resentment, which blocks sexual connection, needs to be dealt with and abandoned. Forgiveness can be achieved through mutual understanding and lots of conversation. Love can be reborn if it has died. But the desire for love must be acknowledged. It must be desired and it must be worked at after many years of life together.

What is true for a couple is indeed true for self, as well. Many people fall out of love with themselves and spend their final years beating themselves up for past follies, failures and infidelities. In order to embrace another, or to embrace your future with passion and peace, it is vital that you forgive yourself and dance with your own mystery. You are a gracious gift for the world and not just some nuisance that you have to put up with.

As we age, it seems we become more androgynous. The physical differences that marked our gender slowly fade. The Gospel of Thomas states that the kingdom of God cannot be achieved until the male becomes female and the female becomes male. This last gift of time is a period of life for that fullest dance.

Women in our generation have developed strong masculine energy as well as feminine energy. But many males have been frightened by anything female (including women!). This is a time for men to develop those virtues, typically seen as female: compassion, nurturing, conversation, receptivity, beauty. Men seem to be less threatened by these qualities as they age. It always amazes me how macho men break through when their grandchildren seduce them into recovering that lovely energy that their workplaces suppressed and forbade in their earlier years.

It is a time to go beyond the gender you have been given. You will always be that gender. But there is more to each of us than our gender definition. As we approach the grave, something happens to us. Many of our body parts begin to sag as the body readies itself to return to the earth. Men and women are sometimes hard to distinguish (sans makeup). More and more we become alike in our physical nature. This is an excellent time to explore the inner dynamics of the other within ourselves. How sad to think that most of us die with so little growth in this area due, often, to convention or lack of imagination or fear.

When an old man confessed to me years ago, that he had sexual fantasies, I stunned him when I congratulated him rather than rebuked him. I want, like him, to die living …

Laughter

He who laughs, *lasts!*

I read that on a bumper sticker some time ago and thought that it contained great wisdom. Humour, from the Latin word, *humor*, means liquid. It is the main ingredient for flexibility. When I look at the races that have survived well in the past generations, I am always called to look upon the Jews, the Aboriginals, the North American Blacks and the Irish. All four groups were called, by circumstance, to be nomadic. They faced unbelievable challenges. Holocaust, famine, shipwreck, persecution, addiction and removal of their religion, language and culture. How did they survive? With courageous laughter, jokes, and song. They have been the mainstay of North American culture. Our theatre is anchored in the residue of the tragic.

Smiling and laughing exercise fifteen facial muscles which, in turn, cause us to breathe in a fuller manner. Even the air in a room changes with laughter. And it is contagious!

I was invited once to speak about humour to the managers of all the bowling alleys in Canada, in the city of Montreal. The title I gave my presentation was, "Thought I'd die laughing!" I was all excited about it until my agent told me that the previous year, they had brought in a comedian from the United States. They had high expectations for this keynote presentation for their association's congress. I was terrified. I thought *I'd die*! I had planned a good but somewhat cerebral look at humour in the workplace. There were analysis, a psychological aspect and some practical ways to use humour in the work setting.

I'm not sure what transformed the session, but when I appeared in front of them, their desire for fun changed me. I was charged! I abandoned most of my intellectual material and as I presented, we laughed, and laughed, and laughed.

Humour can transform the most debilitating conditions into positive spaces for growth.

Practice humour. Watch funny shows. Read the *funnies*. We are never too old to enjoy that sort of thing. Spend time with people who dare to laugh. The dour should be avoided at all cost. If you only have two or thirty years left, don't waste your time with those who have already opted for death. They won't likely miss you and won't want *your kind* to bring in your *Babette's Feast* to disturb their serenity. Surround yourself with a few spicy people who have chosen joy over sorrow. Find places where that kind of person gathers and go there. Or invite them into your life.

I have met many people in their seventies and eighties in bereavement groups. Some moan endlessly about their loss. The ones who survive a loss best seem to be the ones who have been able to infuse some humour into their life. They don't deny the grief and utter sadness, but they sprinkle it with humour and pull themselves and others out of the stew of sadness. They see the ridiculous energy of "hanging on" to anything. They realize that we are not in control.

People with absolute seriousness embrace that myth. The sane person is one who is willing and able to "let go" and to realize that life is gift, people are gifts and that the practice of flexibility and *humour* can bring contentment. Would we ever, for a moment, believe that anyone or anything is *forever*? Indeed, it is their passing by that makes them so valuable.

In one grief session I was leading, many years ago, there was a spicy old Scottish woman who bemoaned the fact that many of her colleagues in the retirement home were insisting that, after two months of grieving the death of her husband, she should "get over" him.

I asked her how long she and her husband had been together. She said that it was fifty-five years.

I asked her if she liked him. She adored him. I then suggested that she might not *want* to get over him. She could still enjoy a relationship with him. Grieving was appropriate. Two months was a very short time. She had to get used to everything from sleeping alone to eating alone and to being in charge of all aspects of her life. She was a happy woman and she seemed, to me, to be doing quite remarkably well.

I suggested that she tell her friends to "buzz off." She simply needed the support from someone to do that. So, one day, as she was shopping at a local bazaar, she came across a woman who had cross-stitched a sign that read "buzz off." She bought it and with her Scottish wit, wore it to the next gathering with the friends. They got the point. She had a great laugh about it.

The Blues

Even cowboys get the blues. Yeah, even cowgirls. So do comedians. So do psychiatrists. Indeed, everyone who lives and breathes is both a victim of and graced by this phenomenon.

In this last period of time, humans seem, at times, to be invaded by sad energy. It comes at the most unexpected times. It sometimes intrudes on what seemed to be a good day. But it comes both in the light of day and in the shadows of evening.

This is normal.

We fall into depressed states, generally when our emotions and our reason are out of step with each other, when passion can't dance with our reason. We seem to get stuck in an in-between state.

Age seems to gather phantoms. Old scripts, old negative thought patterns, even old attitudes that we hated in our parents sometimes overtake us. Events that were forgotten, people we entwined with, places we would never want to visit again, at times come back with crystal clarity and knock us off balance.

And we go into a slump.

For some of us, there has been severe damage — even physical — that causes our system to react in sadness, anger or hostility. Sometimes that energy is directed towards others, even dead others. Often it is directed to our own being. What can we do?

Well, we can stew. Some do. They stay isolated. They stay stuck. They believe that this is their destiny and take that identity on as if it were their spouse. Some even become addicted to their sadness and wear it as a mourner's black gown.

Or, we can decide that this is a state of imbalance and unhappiness that can be remedied. In depression, there is no one way that will work for everyone. From Gestalt to Cognitive Behaviour Therapy to Jungian Dream Analysis to Prozac, there are hundreds of approaches available to help relieve this condition. No one way is guaranteed to work for any one person. The secret is to *start somewhere.*

It is here that the movement to grow somewhere is triggered. What appears to be a glitch in the life pattern could turn out to be the key to new and improved living. Invariably, the dark time was triggered by imbalance. This happens all the time in our body systems. We suffer, get help and improve. Why not in the land of the emotions and reason?

As a first step, acknowledge that you are ill at ease, that you are in pain, that you feel out of kilter. For some, that is a tremendous step, especially if they have been feeling down for so long that this condition feels normal. Some have been numbed to the reality of pain and discomfort.

Next, get words for what is wrong. Say them out loud. Write them down. Tell someone else. This could take a long time and demand some energy that you've blocked. Or you could have been bred to believe that you should *not feel that way about anything.* But you do. So, deal with it.

Next, find someone you can trust to hear you out. It might be your friend, a trusted colleague, a rabbi, priest or minister, a therapist. Find someone who can listen and honour your pain.

Don't stay stuck in your thoughts. Move, act, exercise non-rational behaviour. I was able to help an old man in a psychiatric hospital come out of a twenty-year blockage through a finger-painting exercise. I have seen people unplug from their sadness through intense breathing, or the acceptance of pleasure. I have witnessed people recover their spirit through exercise, playing with an animal, holding a newborn baby, or dancing to music.

Change your reckless ways of thinking. You might have to spend energy and money on getting help to rid yourself of unhealthy thought patterns that negativize reality. Very often the negative moods, feelings and reactions you have to reality come from old attitudes or approaches to life that you didn't even realize you had.

We *were* carefully taught. We can be carefully liberated. You decide.

Walk

It's cheap. It's easy. And everyone in the world does it — except for most of us in North America.

Likely the greatest source of disease in our civilization is due to the fact that we don't walk. We have abdicated what is most native to us in honour of the motor vehicle.

I try to walk for at least an hour daily, most days of the week. On my sixtieth birthday I vowed to myself that I would take better care of myself. I decided that life could have a different flavour if I were to be more proactive in my health.

I can remember as a child, the healthiest older people I knew walked. Elizabeth was a librarian who lived in our neighbourhood. Every day this matronly looking woman, who was from England, walked by our house wearing a tweed suit and sensible Oxford shoes. Every day. She strutted. She always seemed to be enjoying herself. And every day she saw us, with a smile on her face and rosy cheeks, she would grant us a gracious, "Good morning" and continue on her way. All I remember is the icon that she became. I am told that she lived to be a great old woman.

I loved to walk as a kid. I would often go to my friends' doors and ask if they wanted to come for a walk with me. Very seldom did I get a positive response. "Why would you want to go for a walk?" they asked. I have always loved to do it, but sometimes, in my own history, forgot that I enjoyed it.

So, in these past years, I have begun the exercise of walking as a spiritual exercise for my self. Often, at the beginning of the walk, I feel sluggish and have to push myself. But once I start, I am surprised how much I enjoy it. I find it better for me to allow myself *at least* an hour. Otherwise, I don't permit myself enough time to "let go." And every time I feign lack of time, I remind myself that it is one-twenty-fourth of a day. Can't I afford that little time to feed myself? There is always enough time.

Sometimes it means getting up an hour earlier, if I have to go to town that day. I can go to bed an hour earlier and forget the ten o'clock news. In fact, in our household, we always say that we "turn on the ten o'clock news and then wake up and go to bed." Why not short-cut all that, and just go to bed?

I have a few paths I follow, but generally, I try to stick to one or two. It is exciting to see how the same geography changes at different times of the day, different seasons and in different weather conditions. I become aware of new realities both within and outside me that surface in the rain or the snow. Whoever said that, because it is raining or snowing, you cannot go for a walk? My internal geography is affected by the external geography. Different conditions stir up different reflections on my walks.

The greatest benefit of going for *extended* walks comes from the fact that there is "too much time." It is the practice of "too much time" that is important for our growing somewhere. There could be days, weeks even years when there will be too much time. It is important, when we are in health, to prepare for those days and nights. If we don't know how to dance with this reality, we will live in sadness and likely contaminate others with our sadness.

Now and again, I propose a theme to my walk time. One day, for example, I might spend the time reflecting on the *blessings* of my life. They are innumerable.

I then have the time to remember events/people/gifts that came to me and enhanced my days and nights on this earth. I have never been unable to fill up an hour with blessings.

At various times, I have had friends who were going through a rough patch. I walk for them. I send the energy that the walk takes and gives, and direct it to my friends. I am sure it helps. Energy is energy. It does not dissipate. It goes somewhere. I believe I can direct it. Now and again I'll tell a friend that I am doing this for them. It gives them great courage and it encourages me to do something that, at times, I find challenging.

Sometimes I will direct the energy of the walk towards some global issue: ecology, war and peace, concord.

As I age and prepare to re-integrate with the *whole* of the universe, this is an important gesture of deepest compassion. I cannot possibly undo the savagery of the world, nor can I prevent tragedy. But I can send out compassionate energy that could have a tremendous effect in the world. It could possibly influence the world. It will certainly position me for peace and harmony.

I find that the time I allot to walking every day, offers me the time to scan my life. As in my computer, the scanning energy unearths viruses. Stuck in the cracks of my memory lie events and people that need to be dealt with. They often represent moments that I lived through with great pain. They carry the energy of conflicts, hatred, fear, unresolved relationships and confusion. I need to forgive them in order to live in a free manner. Most of the time, these issues arise out of nowhere. I did not call them up. They were simply scanned and appear from the past. I use this time of walking to deal with them. I acknowledge them, get words for them, recover feelings about them and thus begin the work of forgiving them.

I also ask forgiveness for the things I have done to confuse peoples' lives.

Sometimes I walk to engage *imagination.* I find that in the process of emptying my mind of static, I enter into a time I would never have been able to plan. It is a way to enter into *kairos* time, which takes me beyond *kronos,* or ordinary time. It is an invitation to other dimensions of ourselves that we generally don't bother to embrace, or are unaware of. They are inevitably part of us, and can seep into our consciousness and take us on a new adventure.

Sometimes I walk *just for the hell of it*. It is beautiful. It is refreshing. And it is good for my health — both physically and spiritually. My senses awaken to horizons I've been numb to in my *busy* time.

Food

Nothing accompanies our human journey the way food does. It is our friend. It gives zest to our days and nights and surrounds every major event in our life. Now and again it becomes a danger for us, but only because we have abused its generous being.

Choose food that has beauty, freshness and health. Choose food, first of all, that is local and seasonal. It can help you be *in synch* with the seasons and provide you with important nutrients to support your health.

Food preparation can be a transforming activity. Take time to prepare it.

Most people, at one time or another, will have to fend for themselves. Everyone *can* cook. If you have depended exclusively on another person to prepare food for you all your life, you should consider how you will survive when the *cook* dies. Many go into a deep depression when this accustomed source of nourishment is gone. You would be wise to prepare for your own survival. The *cook* might appreciate your developing an interest as well! And it can help you appreciate not only the one who has looked after you all these years, but might also help you appreciate *food* better.

Food is a gift. It does not just appear. It needs to be grown in our gardens or on our balconies, or purchased, prepared, arranged, served and eaten.

Take time to eat. Food can be a source of great enjoyment and spiritual growth. But for that, it requires that you savour it, look at it, smell it, taste it. To devour it rapidly shows disrespect for the food, the cook and for your own body.

There is a *slow movement* growing internationally that is encouraging people to do just that. Take time. We have been seduced by *fast foods* and *prepared foods*. Most of them are so laden with additives that they cannot possibly support our health. They may give you time at this end of your life but they might rob you of time at the final end.

Healthy eating requires healthy table etiquette. That requires, first of all, a table or some respected place for meals.

Allow time to set the table — even if you live alone. Take time to make the setting pleasant. Use the good cutlery — even for yourself. Put a cloth on the table, flowers, candles. Even for yourself. If you don't take time to appreciate a meal, you may not be bothered taking time with other aspects of your life. You are worthy of this. Don't save it for when the guests come. Treat yourself as an honoured guest. Even for breakfast. Establish some rituals around your daily bread.

Some of the healthiest and happiest people I know live alone. Most of them have bothered to bother with themselves. A glass of wine with a meal. Time set aside to value the food. A setting that is welcoming. Music to accompany the meal. Grace before and after meals. These activities can help provide nourishment beyond the valuable nutrients.

Try to avoid doing many things when you eat. When you partake of a meal, partake of a meal. Television or the news on radio can, perhaps, keep you company while you eat. But the food can become a condiment to the main course — the medium that has seduced you. Is the food not valuable enough to merit your full attention? If it is not, then take some cooking lessons from someone and spruce up your humanity.

Try recipes out on yourself and then invite others to partake with you.

⸙ ⸙ ⸙

Jim had been well looked after by Dolores, his wife of thirty years. She died quite suddenly from a stroke at the age of fifty-six. Jim prided himself on being unable even to boil water. He went into a deep slump after Dolores's death. His kids tried to look after him as best they could. But they all had lives to live and small children to think about. Neither he wanted to live with them nor did they want to have him in their homes all the time.

It took about six months of macaroni and cheese and take-out food to begin to affect his health. He put on a tremendous amount of weight and became susceptible to every virus in town. Dolores had assured him and the family of well-rounded, nutritional meals. He missed the tasty food, the table rituals that she had provided at every meal. She set the table at night for breakfast the following morning. She always invested in time and beauty in their mealtimes. Jim felt abandoned on many levels. And it showed.

One of his best supports in this difficult time was a good life-long friend, Mark. Mark's wife detested cooking, so the task of meal preparation was Mark's. He had developed a knack for it and enhanced his native talent by watching television cooking programs.

He had become a very good cook and took great pride in it. One day he offered Jim a quick and easy survival course in cooking. Jim was reluctant at first — especially because he considered it a woman's domain. But somehow the idea caught and he began to enjoy food preparation. He got out Dolores's favourite old recipes and discovered that it was not beyond his capabilities to prepare a meal. In fact, he did just as well as she had!

The real treat came when he invited his children and their spouses and kids for a Sunday dinner. "Stupendous, Dad, when did you ever learn to do this? Now you can cook for us!"

Do you think Jim will spend the rest of his life alone? This new-found gift will likely spill over into new and strong relationships. If he were ever to connect with a new spouse, chances are that he would share in meal preparation. He has discovered great power in the ordinary.

Food also opens up to us *the other.* There are great lessons to be learned in becoming acquainted with foods from other lands. People who seemed foreign to us can become acquaintances and even friends through acquaintance with their foods. Most cities in the world have a panoply of restaurants. In most cities you could eat in a different cultural restaurant daily. Why not become expansive? You could become friendly with the proprietors, the wait staff, the food and drink and through them all, the culture. There is a big world out there that beats meat and potatoes. As racism dissolves when the *unknown* becomes *familiar*, fears can turn to delight when we become comfortable with the *other*.

Food also creates a link with our own cultural and family traditions. It is a great legacy to pass on recipes that have journeyed from one generation to another in your family. Adults crave the tastes of their youth. I can still smell my mother's pies. I still yearn for some of the foods that my aunt prepared so lovingly for us when we visited. I treasure their cookbooks and the stories that accompany many dishes.

My Aunt Marjorie possessed the family recipe for Christmas Cake. Others made fruit cakes at Christmas but no one was able to make *her* cake. It was her cake that was distributed among her family. It was the cake that was served on Boxing Day when the friends and neighbours would visit when I was a child.

My aunt has been *dying* every year for the past number of years, as she is getting older. Yet, she is still with us. Every year, for the past five or six, when the cake would arrive, I found that I was treasuring it more and more. In fact, I was hoarding it. Because she was in her eighties, I feared that losing the last piece of cake would be losing her. I would hold on to the last piece until Easter.

Then I began to realize that she made the cake to be eaten and enjoyed. To hoard it was not to respect either the food or her wishes. So I ate the last piece.

However, I did approach her for the recipe. She

gave it lovingly and then went with me to the market (which we did yearly, in the fall) and purchased the fruits and nuts for the cake. Then we proceeded to make it. I made it under her expert supervision.

I have received many gifts from my elders who have died. But perhaps the one I most appreciate is that cake. Surely I will pass it on, as well. Food carries energy, stories and promise.

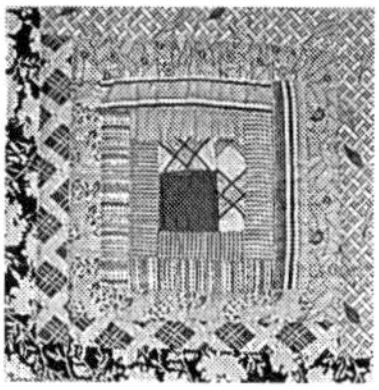

3

Imagination — Designing Your Future

> When I've looked at life, I've seen it as if it were like frogs jumping from lily pad to lily pad, and it's as if, when we get older, the lily pads get farther apart, and sometimes we land on some rocks, and sometimes we fall in.
>
> — *Matthew Harsant, age 10 (upon reviewing his father's career planning information in 1985)*

What time is it now?

Sell everything and rent? Continue to work? Travel?

Suddenly, the other day I awoke to the fact that I am sixty-three. I began writing this book in my fifties. Now I'm sixty-three! From the introduction there have been lots of changes. Some of the people in the dedication are dead. Our dog, Morgan, is dead. New things have happened to me since I first put my hands on the keyboard. It's not even the same keyboard.

My parents died before they were fifty. My step-dad retired at sixty-two and died at eighty. That's pretty good for a male. He enjoyed his eighteen years of freedom. I am sixty-three. In seventeen years I will be eighty. I remember seventeen years ago as though it were yesterday. *Tempus fugit.*

We always speak of a great realization that comes to us at forty, when we realize that all our goals haven't been reached. It is a capital time for re-assertion, re-direction and all the other "re's." But at forty, I lived with the illusion that there were fifty or so years ahead. In fact, it felt that there was an eternity of time left in which to accomplish all my dreams and goals. Now there are seventeen, if I am lucky. Maybe more … maybe less.

What will I do in these last years? Work till I'm in my seventies and have a few years for leisure? Or work until I drop from some illness that will incapacitate me until I die? Will we stay here in the country, or downsize like most of our contemporaries do? Should we be in the city and closer to the big hospitals, or are we not well enough served by our local doctor and small hospital where we are known and respected? As I converse with many of my contemporaries, these are the new questions that bombard our minds as we face the future.

The main issue is: what do you want to do with the time left? Have you done what you want to do? Can you? What do you choose to engage in? What do you have to forego? How do you embrace the future in such a way that *you* direct the last gift of time — as much as you can, anyway?

For the first time in my life, I am bothered, terrified and intrigued by the fact that there is an end in view. Never before have I consciously begun to count the springs and summers or wonder about the number of vacations that remain. There are so many things to see and do in such a short space of time — things I can design or manipulate and others that are beyond my powers.

I could remain healthy until the end. Or I might be struck with something or other, any day now. I recovered from prostate cancer a few years ago, like so many my age. I question what my health will look like in the years to come, beyond what I can do to maintain it.

I'm doing all in my power to stay healthy. I have a personal trainer who comes to the house. I follow a low fat, high fibre diet. I snowshoe almost every winter day. I walk the rest of the year. I get adequate sleep. I drink a glass of red wine a day. I even eat dark chocolate. I'm told that all this will prolong my life a bit more! I am in an excellent relationship. They say that prolongs life, as well. I even make and eat chicken soup, which my Jewish friends assure me will keep me in good health.

But there could be unforeseen enemies that come — out of the blue. They could even turn out not to be *enemies*, but *friends* that make me holy and wise and, ultimately, *fulfilled*. I have known so many who were attacked by some disease, or had an accident that turned their lives around in a positive way — although these things were perceived as *enemies* at the time of their arrival.

How do you decide what priorities to choose for the next period of time? What will your life look like in this last gift of time? Who can you possibly be after the life you have known is no longer possible, or desired? Your *jobs* have defined you for most of your life. Is there a life after work? After the children have gone? After your spouse has departed?

What time is it in your life? Here are some ideas. I hope they help you work it out.

Wonder

"Sometimes I sits and thinks. And sometimes I just sits." I remember seeing that on a banner once. I found it amusing. From my childhood, I was programmed to *do*. Just sitting was idle. "An idle mind is the devil's workshop," I was told.

But an idle mind is also God's workshop — or my workshop — or anyone's workshop. There is nothing wrong with that. Most of us have been programmed to be always busy and to disallow any spirit unrelated to work entering into our mind and being.

There are normal moments of wondering that occur in our lives. They are times that are offered to us.

But if we are not programmed to accept them, we are as oblivious to them as to the inner *howlings* of our body when they announce that our health is in danger. Sometimes, these moments of awakening are given to us when we are in isolationist mode. Or when the medication hasn't yet clicked in. Or when we are groggy. Or when we have hours or days of sadness. They are indeed offering us a time to be doing nothing. At those times, let your mind fill up with whatever it fills up with. These spirits are coming to you for a reason. Let them.

I was always taught that I was in charge of my imagination and my will. Carl Jung expresses the opposite when he says, "There are things in the psyche which I do not produce but which produce themselves and have their own life." Often, they are messages from afar, or from the past, or maybe from the future. Or, as Jung says, "… from somewhere altogether unknown to me."

Sometimes the inability to *do*, out of fatigue, sluggishness, illness or sadness can open up new horizons. Why fill these moments with *activities*? Why not allow them to unfold in their own time?

To wonder is to gracefully accept the time that is before you without fighting it. Let your imagination run wild. Let reason sleep for a while. Listen to the voices that dance into your imagination, and dance with them before you decide to *change partners*, or go back to your solitude. You could find some new muses who present you with a future you had never dreamed of in your *rational* state.

As a young man, I was always told to control my emotions and my imagination in honour of left-brain, male thinking. Daydreaming was looked upon as lost and wasted time. I was taught, both at home and especially at school, to control any *flights of fancy.*

I say daydream. Use your imagination. Fly fancy-fully!

At last, at this stage of life, free from others' scripts for you, you can bask in your own gifts, which go far beyond what reason can offer. There is lots of time for reason and control. But the time to wonder is a great gift and yours for the asking.

In my youth, I yearned to be "all grown up." What a difference it would make, I thought, to be able to decide and do for myself — without *them*. I also lived in a society that suggested one was to be "grown up" by the time one left home, around the age of eighteen to twenty. One's mind was to be made up about most realities and then one simply had to live within the context of those principles for what remained of life.

That life-vision blocked growth. We will never be "all grown up." Our imaginations can constantly come to life until the day we die. And then, at that point, perhaps that is where we go — into imagination. There is so much exploring to do.

Sometimes in the past few years I have been disturbed by some unusual bodily reaction that I have not experienced before. Shortness of breath, poor sex, blurred eyesight, aches, pains. They have stopped me short and put me into a state of wonder. Am I all right? Am I dying? *Is this it?* What if I can't work some day? What happens when my generation starts to die off, when I am the last one left? If I have a stroke?

In these times, I seem to enter into a new kind of space. It is not chronological or "clock" time, but non-logical time. *Kairos* time, not *kronos* time.

We are offered *kairos* time constantly in our lives. It is bigger than chronological time. It is the time of myths, of deep imagination, of the mystical. It is the kind of "let's pretend" time that we entered into when we were children playing cops and robbers, cowboys, house, school. We did not *just* pretend but we *actually became* the new time. It was a bigger time and a much more interesting space in which to dwell. Strange, isn't it, that we generally disallow that kind of time to enrapture us after the age of ten?

It is an opportunity for us to go beyond the now and to experience *deeper being.* Usually we try to pull ourselves out of that space, pull up our socks and *get real.* But we must not forget that these moments are invitations to the *really real*. We have experienced *glimpses* of this kind of reality in our youth. Now we may discover that there is more … much more.

We are invited into this time in some of the *ordinary* events that come our way. Christmas, Hanukkah, reunions, funerals, liturgy, meals, sexual experiences. But more often than not, we stay on the outside and fear to enter in. It is hard for us to let go of the rational and enter into the realm of the imagination — even in poetry or dance or music or art. But we are constantly invited in. We know that there is more to life than meets the eye, but in our culture we have been bred to dismiss it as unreal or unworthy of adults. Thank God for children who sometimes invite us to become who we really are.

A few years ago, a friend's five-year-old invited me to descend to the depths of our old Edwardian Toronto home's basement to play hide and seek. I assured him that no one had been down there since the early nineteen-hundreds. But he insisted and I caved in. He invited me into a world I had forgotten. In it, time disappeared. We were *in the moment* and it was a very dense and energetic moment that had nothing to do with three o'clock or four. We were in a timeless state that I knew I knew but had long forgotten. I began to enjoy the experience the little boy offered me. He invited me into a realm that I loved as a child. It offered me hope and expansiveness and joy. I remember leaving that experience and thinking, "Couldn't I go there *without* a five-year-old?" Why did it take his dive into the fanciful to get me there? Had I forgotten some basic instinctual aspect of my being human? Indeed, I had. And truly, I could go there on my own steam. I just had to *dare*!

At Christmas in our home we always have crackers at the dinner table. At the beginning of the meal, we break open the crackers, redeem the gifts that are enveloped in the brilliant paper, read the fortunes that come to us and put on the paper crowns.

It is always interesting to see who can readily put on the paper hat, and who cannot. The kids do it with no hesitancy. Many of the adults do it reluctantly. It means, "We are going to *play* now." We are entering into a ritual time. This is a ritual meal with ritual foods and *filled* with memories and imagination. In the meal we are linked not only to every Christmas meal we've ever eaten but to every table that is celebrating like this, everywhere. There are ritual foods — turkey or some other winged fowl, cranberry sauce, plum pudding, Christmas fruit cake. These are constants in every festival at this time of year. It would not be Christmas for many, without them.

Or we can just eat dinner.

Today I snowshoed. It was -20°C. I went *there* again. It was a mystical trip into the beyond. Timeless, spaceless and beckoning …

The snow was deep and had been refreshed by gusts of wind that blew across the hills. The sun hit the snow and it sparkled like diamonds. It brought back memories of my childhood. It actually linked both times, indeed transcended time and space and took me to a place — beyond words, beyond reason — where I did nothing but admire. I remember how I would sit and look at the sparkles as a child. It was a mystical awakening — at six and at sixty-three. The sparkle made me one with everything in the universe.

My friend Ron was dying with leukemia several years ago. I remember helping him prepare for death. He had been a very successful orthodontist. Despite the fact that he worked incessantly and took few vacations, he seemed to live a life of exemplary healthiness. He was an avid runner. He ran with a passion — almost addictively. He would go out in the early morning and run for miles and miles. He also ran major marathons.

He often spoke to me about the space he encountered when running — a mystical, sacred place he entered. He acknowledged it. He loved it. He ran to go there. He told me that it was a place where peace and quiet dwelt, where there was no worry, no time, no clutter.

When he was confined to bed and readying himself for departing this life, he often felt sad, guilty, lost and afraid. I invited him to "go to that sacred place, to remember that *kairos* time, to embrace it and sweetly dwell in it." It was where my friend was king, where he was his truest self, his divine child. His bliss. It would be a foretaste of who he would be and a glimpse of who he had always been. It didn't cost anything. It didn't need to be acquired or searched out. It was within him.

Fortunately, he had been able to experience this aspect of his being before his death called. He had grown into his inner self and was familiar with his innermost secret self. At times, the pain and the unknown overwhelmed him. But he kept going to the place of his *king*, day after day. At last, he entered into the *kairos* time once again, in his death.

We are inclined to dismiss these kinds of moments as unreal. We should be careful, for we are possibly missing the greatest opportunity for our human development offered to us in life. This is not an additive, or a supplement to who we are. It is of our essence. *"L'important, c'est la rose."* It is often the invisible, the unseen, that frees us.

Now is the time to scour the universe! Do you remember, as a child, you wondered at the life of the ants that led such an intriguing life in the sand and cracks of the sidewalk? Do you remember how you spent hours watching, wondering, creating scripts that they lived by? Time flowed by. It was full of wonder.

But how often I have passed by the small things that might transport me to a plane where I could be, yet just don't *bother*? How my life could be transformed if I would pay attention to wonder.

Take time every day to sit or to walk. Try to empty your mind of everything that compels you. Breathe. We are not accustomed to do this, so it can be difficult. Get away from the phone and the desk. Create a space for yourself. Possibly you will need a quiet corner in your home, or on your property, in a park or in a place of worship. Don't be threatened by silence and by unanticipated lulls in life. Turn off the radio in your life and just listen.

The Church of the Holy Trinity, in the heart of

downtown Toronto, has created a huge labyrinth in the park beside the church and the shopping mall. It offers a haven for people who work in the office towers that surround it. At noon, after work — even on their breaks throughout the day — people walk the labyrinth in silence. It is a true oasis in the desert.

A short while ago, I spent a day working with a group of nurses at Ash Croft. Our subject was "burnout." I had a program worked out for them with lots of theory, group work, private reflection and more. They arrived from the city in a dither. Some were held up by terrible traffic heading out of the city. There had been a threat of a storm. They were a mess. Still, they were anxious to get going with the program that they had anticipated for quite some time. They knew they were in desperate need. Most nurses are.

I looked at them and made a deep compassionate decision. We would begin the morning with a long, silent walk through the property.

We walked the paths and stopped at various points for reflection and for quiet listening. It took at least an hour out of our planned schedule. I was anticipating that the A-types would be upset. On the contrary, the overwhelming feeling of the group at check-in was that it was the silence that was the teacher. They exclaimed that they seldom experienced silence and quiet. They did not appreciate its value until that point.

It would now become an important ingredient in their mental and physical health program.

It was in entering into the *unaccustomed* that they discovered the *normal*, which had been numbed in them. They were able to receive the energy that they needed so much in their healing work in the core of a big city. Now they could bring breath and *élan vital* to their clients and to their own life. They just had to remember the experience. Many of them took some branches, pine cones, snail shells, stones or images with them that would feed their lives with hope. Those items could put them back into the experience, even in the midst of chaos.

Reality is full of wonder, if we take the time.

Creativity

I was attending our local Arts Council's monthly meeting a while ago at a nearby restaurant. A friend of mine was the speaker after lunch. He had been a professor of economics until his *retirement*.

Never having absorbed that word into his vocabulary, he pursued his beloved gardening, to the point of *living* gardening. In the thirty years that he has been planning his garden, he has become one with the land in the Mulmur Hills to the north of our land. He spoke to us about how he had transformed the acres that surround his century farmhouse. To hear how the acres around his farmhouse transformed *him* was even more delightful. It was not just a question of what could grow where, but how diverse plants would fit into the landscape, enhancing what was already there, giving each new flower, shrub or tree new grace.

Thomas Aquinas states so emphatically that "grace enhances nature." Grace does not *change* nature. Nature is good. What we simply do is enhance something that is already valid. Being is good. Being, graced with a presence, is enhancing both for the beheld and for the beholder. What my friend does in his garden is *co-creative* activity. He enhances the created order. And it is good.

So too, are you — in the many things that you are called to do every day. What is it you do that *graces* the nature around and within you?

It could start with what you put on first thing in the day. A colour that enhances you. An outfit that becomes you. A scent that recollects you. Or it could be how you manage a work project. Or the way you gather with friends.

Use your imagination in all you do. You could have meat and potatoes or you could have *escalope de veau avec ...*, which might not cost more, take any more time to prepare, but would take you to another level.

Or you could do take-out.

When I was living in downtown Toronto a few years ago, I remember seeing a retired judge. I don't know his name but I knew he had been a judge. His image is as clear as a bell to me. Every morning at seven-thirty this elderly gentleman would wander out of our fashionable condominium wearing his Harris tweed jacket, a shirt and a natty tie, handsome trousers and walking shoes, a tweed cap and his walking stick. I think he was at least eighty years old. Every morning he was a living icon of hope for me as he paraded out the door, up to the gardens at St. James Cathedral and off into the distance. I would see him return a few hours later — having transformed the neighbourhood with his presence.

He could have stayed in bed. Instead, he brought the very breath of life to our effervescent neighbourhood as it woke up. Imagine the number of younger men and women he acknowledged. He was prone to say "Good morning" to those he passed, with a smile on his wrinkled face. Imagine how they marvelled at his energy, his dignity and his joy. I am sure he transformed their walk into a prance.

At any moment of our life, you can decide to *grow* with the created order of things. The alternative is to buck growth by passively hanging back. You can decide to *engage*. This activity takes a constant refocusing. The rewards are stupendous.

I am always surprised when, after a period of numbness (usually after I have been writing for awhile and I begin to feel listless), I can conjure up enough energy to force myself to go for a walk. I struggle with the concept. Either it is too cold and I have to bundle up, or it is too warm and I have to face sweating, or it is just too much to fathom. I know, however, that if I manage to pull myself out of the pit I have found myself in, I am able to re-awaken myself and return from the walk with a new energy and generally, some crisp, new ideas. Often, I remember that old judge …

I can embrace creation, or I can numb myself to it. Generally, I am not negative enough to deny reality, but I can quite easily just glide beside it all and not acknowledge it. All I have to do is open up.

Branching out

As a boy, I was told in art class that I had painted a sky purple and *not* blue. I will never forget that moment. Perhaps I saw a purple sky, perhaps I thought that purple was blue. I don't know. All I remember is that I was shamed. "Skies are blue," the teacher told me.

All my life, I have lived with a script that says that I am colour-blind. I am not. I don't see colours the way my grade three teacher saw them. But I see colour. And skies are not always blue.

Last summer I decided that I wanted to produce a new CD of piano improvisations. My first CD, *River Ash*, had been successful. Improvisations are interesting. You start with nothing and wait. Sometimes something emerges and you have a product. Sometimes nothing emerges and you have nothing. So you wait. Eventually, you might have a product. The experience of producing my first album was so good that I yearned to open myself up to the unknown and go for it again.

But I was blocked. I couldn't get started. Whatever I did sounded like what I had already done. I decided that I should try to "unblock" my imagination by going down some other road.

In order to do this, I enrolled in an art class directed by the Louisiana artist, Douglas Walton. One of his first principles is: "Right is pedestrian and saleable. What began as wrong often triggers genius and that is what hangs in museums." I soon discovered that skies are blue and red and yellow and pink and purple and, alas, brown.

One of the by-products of my art adventure has been the awakening of the divine artist within me. In the past months, I have hung some of my art in our lovely country home. We don't advertise who did them. It is amazing how many of our very sophisticated friends — some even artists — exclaim how wonderful the new acquisitions are. After awhile, we break down and tell them who actually did paint them. Interestingly enough, I have been accused of being Cézanne, Miro and Matisse. Perhaps, we all entered into the same *imagination*.

I appreciated an article I read on Miles Davis where he stated, with the kind of emphasis that only he could, "Mistakes are part of the music."

These are important insights that I need to know as

an artist of my own life. I am not a mistake. My "mistakes" are not mistakes. They are part of the fibre and texture and pigment of my days.

By taking two weeks "off" to go to these art classes — or rather by taking two weeks "on" — I was able to leave behind my patterns of *rightness and pedestrian* to enter into the realm of the eternal and *awe-full*. It took that step out of the ordinary to allow myself to enter into the extraordinary. Then the music could flow.

I needed to break new ground in order to re-energize the old, too familiar, and too ordered territory. The new CD is taking shape and it's one I didn't expect. It took time, waiting, patience, listening and a willingness to venture into the big picture where the true energy lay.

I think it could be an important message to write on the mirror in your bathroom: "Mistakes are part of the music." Remind yourself that you are the song, not a mistake. You are a piece of marvellous art. You are!

♪♪♪

> I dwelt in a world where nothing was explained to children except the supremacy of the concept of loyalty. I learned from my mother that loyalty was the pretty face one wore when you based your whole life on a series of egregious lies.
>
> *— Pat Conroy, Prince of Tides*

These words resonate on every level of my being as I engage, at post mid-life, in a mission of systemic realignment, an alignment of my soul with itself. The period from birth until truth was a balancing act between the terror of integrity and the niceness of the lies. The act of accepting your own being, after years of hiding in the back staircase of shadow, is an ultimate act of sanctification and of truest birth.

I have met so many in my generation who were never really able to embrace their true being because of some axe that was hanging over them. It made them hide essential characteristics of who they really were and who they might emerge as.

Sometimes the source of their shame was a statement they overheard in their youth, or some proclamation from a parent or superior that invalidated their dream, their personality, their being. Many became extroverted because someone wanted them to be able to sing and dance for everyone. It was only later in life that they were able to embrace *their* gift of introversion. Some declined being this or that because "girls don't do that," or "no one in our family ever did that." So many geniuses stayed in the scullery because their tribe never ventured outside the house.

Many of those people and institutions that shamed us are dead now. For the most part, we have managed to "live around them," or live with some freedom from their judgment or interference. In some cases, however, the largest interference in our own personal development comes from ourselves. Sometimes blockages reflect others' attitudes, but sometimes they are limitations we have put on ourselves out of fear, shame or guilt, perceived societal norms or definitions of "correctness" that we have internally established.

Sometimes, it only takes a new opportunity, a disaster, some creative mentor, a new love — whatever — to pull us out of our limiting cubicles. Often, it is in travelling abroad, in meeting new people, in new job opportunities, in being fired, that we realize the kinds of prisons into which we have put ourselves.

I have European friends who have had to leave their country because they felt hemmed in and unable to express their art outside a specified box. They had to come to a "new world" to be able to express themselves. Most of us need to find a "new world" where our truest self can emerge before death. Some take longer than others. Some never make it. I hope you do.

Many of us need to "leave home" before we can embrace our souls. Many would never dare. We all can and may.

This is a time in your life to experiment with all sorts of challenges. It is smart to have many avenues to travel. Why not dare to try a few things that you've always had a hunch you'd like to do? I have met many people who decided to take up the piano, work in a grocery store, help with the music at church, do housekeeping for someone, visit the sick, run for political office. Many of the ventures that were not possible when you were younger could blossom into an assortment of interesting things to do.

Often, people at this age need to supplement their incomes. There could be a variety of projects that could fill the soul with energy and make money as well. Many people need "just something" to get them out of the house, get them into contact with people and allow them to contribute as wise elders in their communities.

There are always, in our generation, people who were not able to study, because of innumerable circumstances. This is a good time to venture forth — Elderhostel, university continuing education programs, bible study, planned tours.

The song from the musical, Cabaret, says it so well:

> Put down the knitting, the book and the broom … Start by admitting that cradle to tomb, isn't that long a stay …

Life is a cabaret with so much to offer you. Don't sit at home and wait for death.

Excites

It seems as if it were yesterday. As a little boy we had lived in a hotel called The Walker House, in downtown Toronto. In this magical place (did we stay there for a week, a month?) lived a princess. Her name was Barbara Ann Scott. She was the most famous figure skater in the world at that time. We would meet in the elevator and even had dinner together (I remember chicken and blueberry pie). We were given tickets to see her skate with Dick Button at Maple Leaf Gardens. They invited me into a world I had only dreamed of. I wanted to be them. I'm not sure which one. Likely both.

So, as a young Roman Catholic boy, when a Holy Day of Obligation came our way (usually December 6 in the winter), we would be free to take the day off from our public school. I would inevitably go to the skating rink at 11th Street in New Toronto, where we lived at that time. Because all the Protestant kids were in school, I would have the rink almost entirely to myself. I remember going after Mass and staying till supper time. I would skate round and round, twirl, jump, glide, shoot the duck, and dream of being Dick Button and Barbara Ann Scott.

I entered into *kairos* time. My imagination ran wild. It was truly in that time that I embraced a "me" I wanted to become. A skater? Perhaps not, in the end, but a mystic, an artist, a creator.

In my work with older adults, I encounter, time and time again, people who have decided, in a late chapter of their lives, to embrace dreams they had always avoided all their life. Often they had abandoned their truest selves in honour of a relationship. The passion or lust blinded them to their souls. Sometimes it was due to religion, a parental interdict or direction, or an unanticipated pregnancy, work requirement or political disaster. Sometimes, in their youth, they just didn't dare risk the imagined dream.

♪♪♪

I remember the joy that came to me when things that I had ordered with two box tops and twenty-five cents would arrive in the mail. I was a member of the Cisco Kid Club. I had a mask and a neckerchief, just like Cisco. Unfortunately, at that time, Mexico was far away and there was never to be the magical hat that is all too available today.

I also was a member of the Dick Tracy Club and had a ring with a magnifying glass and a ballpoint pen that folded out on a piece of plastic that glowed in the dark. I wore every new item to bed — at least the day they arrived. Imagine the thrill of being able to write under the covers, in the dark. What was it that drew me out of the ordinary into a new plane where I could be bigger than life (at least bigger than the life I lived)?

The *excite* was not about *being* Cisco or Dick but about *being bigger* than I was, venturing into the unknown and avoiding the inevitable. There was life beyond 4th Street in New Toronto.

♪♪♪

I have twin toes. I don't know anyone else who has, but I imagine they are common enough. The two toes that grow beside my big toes are actually joined together mid-way up. Not webbed, but twin. My mother told me that boys with twin toes would go to Europe. I have no idea where that story came from.

I'm not even sure I really knew where Europe was, other than that it was away. But I knew, from an early age, that I would surely go there. Once I learned about Europe (whatever on the map wasn't coloured pink — the colour of the British Empire), I developed a deep desire to go there. The desire was reinforced by my stepfather's stories about living abroad, and the wondrous adventures that the pictures of the National Geographic opened up to me, as Dad's monthly issues arrived regularly.

I always knew that my life would not be pedestrian, that there would be adventure. I also knew that there would be opportunities to explore far-off lands where I could experience life differently. How favoured I was, as well, to be raised in a city where new immigrants arrived, almost daily, bringing with them sounds and foods and smells and dress that would make life more and more exciting. As a little boy, the excitement of "the other" was a tremendous gift that would allow me not to be afraid of going where angels fear to tread.

As we age, we can find so many ways to venture into the untried and yet true. I am always thrilled to see senior citizens who travel, people who continue to learn and who find ways of growing.

Venture into your earliest memories about the things that excited you. There might be imaginative seeds planted in those memories that can help you design an imaginative future. Try to remember "earliest" memories from a period before you were shamed into living other peoples' dreams. This could be your best opportunity to embrace *your own soul*. There is still time to shape your activities to reflect who you really are. You must not short circuit the process. To simply do without the deep reflection, could find you doing what you have always done. As a friend of mine always say, "If you always do what you've always done, you'll always be who you've always been". Enjoy your imagination!

♪♪♪

My friend Ruth told me about her wonderful sister, who, well into her nineties took courses at the university and anywhere else she could learn things. She went places because they opened up new horizons for her. She met new people and delighted in their differences. She made sushi in her nineties, because it was *interesting*. I believe that it was because she stayed interested that she lived in health into her nineties!

♪♪♪

I read about an aboriginal woman from Australia who came to town to visit some friends. It was the first time she had found herself in a "European" building. It was rectangular. She had only been in nature, because she led a nomadic life. In nature, there are no straight lines. She did not know how to be there, in a room with four straight walls, so she stood. She was unaccustomed to being confined, because she was able to wander in any direction at her leisure in the woods.

It is not that nature is out of whack — it is we who created the supposed straight line. It offers us endless other possibilities. Straight lines seem to dominate our sense of design, let alone our sense of living. It is hard for us to know how to think other than in a linear way. How many of us are able to dwell in poetry, abstraction in art or music, or the zany in nature or in our own days and nights? Most of us were raised to follow a *straight and narrow path*, not only in religion, but in work, relationships, clothing and lifestyle, as well. There is nothing wrong with staying that way. I have known countless people who lived contented, sane lives. But often, in times of adjustment, times of awakening, we forget that we may take other paths.

In-between times are good times for you to dare to colour outside the lines, listen for another drummer, to choose to wear the colours that convention forbade. Take off the tie and the suit. Risk going to work in a foreign country as a volunteer. Change the furniture. Even move it around. Work in another room. Sleep in the guest room for a while. Dye your hair. Don't dye your hair. Get some …

I enjoy working with a laptop computer. The laptop allows me to change places and write in a variety of rooms and, even better, in clement weather, to write out of doors. Sometimes, all it takes to unblock me is to move to another space for a few hours. My mind and body are refreshed by the change. Sometimes, all it takes is the movement to pull me from boredom and lethargy to brilliance.

Often, the best way for me to get out of a slump is to snowshoe in the winter or to go for a walk. Even a half-hour walk can make me a new man. Inevitably, during that walk, new ideas spring up, or sour ideas fade away. Anger, boredom, resentment and fear can disintegrate by simply changing the scenery, whereas, in the box, the static continues and the discord goes round and round and round.

Avoid toxicity. Some people should be let go. Others should be allowed in. I have held on to people and institutions for years, who did nothing but pull me down. There is no rule that says you have to stay in the mud when all it takes is a pair of good tires to get you out of those spots. Arm yourself with some self respect and let go. Get rid of relics of those people or items that might haunt your house — photos, gifts, music clothing — whatever makes them present to you. Often they keep you from following the paths that could bring new energy your way.

Herbert Otto said that change and growth take place when a person dares to become involved in *experimenting with his or her own life.* The energy needed to do that was experienced in your very early days, in some of those primitive *excites*. If you have blocked a future for yourself, get help to discover what needs to be ripped away, so that you may be set free. Perhaps there are strong messages from your past that squelch any fun, adventure or wonder in you. Demolish the walls that shroud a beautiful *you*, who has sadly been encased in shame.

You are worthy. You can do things, go places, make friends. If you have measured out the mornings, afternoons and evenings of your life in coffee spoons, change. You can stay stuck. Or you can learn to fly like an eagle!

4

Becoming an Elder: Responsibility in the Community and for the Earth

> Humankind is a union of almost infinite diversity. Each person receives some gift from the past and has a gift of new hope to give to the future. The challenge of our time is to offer one another the opportunity to create traditions that will be passed down to future generations.
>
> — *Kamaladevi Chattopadhyay, Resurgence, August,1987*

What is an elder?

Becoming old is a pretty good qualification for being an elder. Age is a very valuable credential for any human being. With it comes understanding, intuition, wisdom and deep perception. Much of that can only come from experience. The years become a trampoline for a valued position in a community.

After the industrial revolution, older adults lost value in the sight of a society that began to value production over life. Older adults got in the way. In fact, they lost the reverence that had been accorded elders in earlier times. Then, older adults had played important roles in society — judges, teachers, priests, rabbis, keepers of the stories, healers and seers.

A hundred years ago, people over sixty-five made up only four per cent of the North American population. Today, about one-seventh of the population in North America is over sixty-five. Most North Americans will live well beyond sixty-five. More and more of us are living longer and longer. *Indeed, we are here!*

So often, I hear reports about our rising numbers. Our potential longevity troubles the powers that be. "Elder care" is a major source of worry for our governments, as it should be. However, I think some of the energy put into worry, should be directed towards an effective use of the great gifts and treasures this generation brings to the earth.

This is not a group of humans to be "let go of" and sent out to pasture. This is a band of energetic, inspired, educated, travelled, spiritual and worldly people full of wisdom, spunk, courage and imagination.

This generation can be a vital bridge between the way things were and the way things are going. This is a generation that still has memory of two centuries ago. The eldest are women and men who lived before the car, the airplane, radio and television. They are people of the land. Many of them are people of many lands. They are an immense treasure.

The eldest of the elders are people who lived through wars, famines, depressions and major civilization shifts. The world they were born into no longer exists except in books and in their vivid stories. They carry tremendous fuel that could ignite the minds and hearts of the next generations. They have suggestions, discoveries, conclusions, wisdom and humour — all elements that are capital in the enhancement of humanity and in the sane and crafty design of our strategies for communal survival and growth.

We still have aboriginal folks who vividly remember living in igloos and hunting for survival — nomads who wandered from place to place, living happily, even joyfully without material goods. We still have people all over the world, who never knew about some of the items we, in this "civilized" world, feel we cannot live without.

We should be listening to them and learning from them. Would we be able to survive without electricity, without the automobile, without prepared foods? We might have to once again. We should not lose the information about survival in the woods, about conversation, about mythology and ritual as a source of spirituality and hope.

Some people attain the state of elderhood only because they became old. Others seem to be anointed with this title at an earlier age. People talk about "old souls." Generally that means that these individuals have been around before. However, I believe that what these people manifest is the gift of wisdom. Wisdom is a deep well from which we all share energy. Some are open to it at an earlier age and become sages for the community. Some stay closed all their lives and only skim the surface of life. It takes all kinds …

The elder embraces wisdom and becomes more and more conscious as the days fly by. Deep consciousness is a gift of aging that can probe profoundly into the past and the present, and embrace positive energy for tomorrow. Wisdom is a treasure that I have found in some generous and gracious older men and women, simply by having conversations with them. It is not the property of the rich and famous, or of the educated. It is gift — a gift to be acknowledged, embraced and grown.

A few years ago, I was taking an acting course at a local university. One of the exercises we were invited to do was centred on "letting go" of all the faces that we put on as mature adults. We ranged in age from twenty to seventy. We asked the children at the Day Care Centre of the university if they would evacuate their playground so that we might play for a bit. We were then invited by the leader to go, one by one, into the play area and let loose for five minutes.

The children were fascinated by the idea that adults might play, and stood outside the fence with their eyes transfixed on the site. We began. Interestingly enough, the first to go was the eldest — a zany old women with lots of zest. She ran into the space, embraced the swings, slides, ropes and all, screamed, yelled, giggled, bellowed and outrageously lived her five minutes. Other, more extroverted members of the group followed. The kids were dumbfounded. They had never seen adults play — at least not like this. We howled. We giggled. We had tears in our eyes and laughter in our hearts.

My turn approached, not because we had an order of participation, but simply there were few left to go. This extrovert becomes very introverted when it comes to this sort of non-conformist behaviour. I wanted to do it. I loved watching everyone else, but I was fearful about doing it myself.

Words, sing-songy words came back to me. "Dare you, dare you. Double dare you!" They came from my youth. I thought of all the challenges that I was called to face as a young boy. Running the race. Jumping over the horse in gym class. Getting the ball in the net. Not hitting the baseball correctly. Catching the baseball when it came my way in centre field. Not having the right response when Brother went up and down the rows asking us the questions from the catechism. Reading when my turn came.

I remember my body in terror. Sweaty hands. Almost wetting my pants out of fear. Eczema on my fingers. Jaw tensed with fear. Gaze directed away from the teacher. The question of daring to do something was daunting for me. Everyone was watching. I could easily fail. They might laugh at me. I might faint. I might look funny.

And here I was once again, this time in my fifties, with the same terror, the same feeling, the same reaction when I was invited to let the "kid" out. Then I heard them say, "Okay, Kelly, it's your turn." I had to go. I felt cornered. And I went.

I did it. I ran into the playground. I yelled, I made funny sounds, I swung on the swings, suspended myself from the ropes, slid down the slides, slithered through the tubes. I tried so hard to have fun. I watched myself make myself have fun. I did it all, all right. They clapped and laughed. I had passed.

But *I* didn't do it!

That would have required that I be *silly.* I had lived with a deep inner message that silly and stupid were synonymous. And I didn't want to be or look stupid. Silly comes from an old English word, *selig*, which in fact means a blessing. I feared acting, in a blessed way, because I feared acting in a stupid way. I realized that day that I had been shamed in my upbringing into behaving *properly.* My fear and terror were actually shame-based and fed.

I have always been impressed by the writings of the Swiss psychiatrist, Alice Miller. In her book, *For Your Own Good: Hidden Cruelty in Child Rearing and the Roots of Violence*, she states that the deepest damage that adults can do to children is to kill their spontaneity.

Most of us were raised with very strong messages that forbade us to take risks that would make us look improper or immature. We were disallowed the freedom and the bliss of doing what comes naturally to us. Our souls were often caged by the spiritual corsets of Victorian propriety, religious fundamentalism or Catholic Jansenism. As a result, only the brave and free dared express their inner truth, and for fear of gross animal behaviour, we forfeited the human in honour of convention and the rule.

We were taught to lie or to hide. To risk offending someone was tantamount to murder in many families. As a result, secrets and lies under-girded most human behaviour. This squelching of the spontaneous in early life prepared us well for the slavery of the reigning culture, religious convention and the economic systems that needed our undivided and faithful support. So we committed suicide spiritually in favour of the safe, the well defined and the appropriate.

To dare to do something. To dare to be someone. To dare to go beyond where we normally dwell is a huge human journey. Most of us were very ill prepared for that kind of dangerous activity. To appear different, to act out of line, to be out of control was forbidden. Never were we encouraged to control anything but our tempers, our emotions, our feelings. Never was there any encouragement to control our reason, our left brain, our work. We had been set up to burn out, to be bored and to die wealthy.

There are so many obstacles in the way of healthy behaviour. Sometimes they are local and tangible and real. But often they are ghosts from our past that keep us from ever going beyond old and hitherto strongly incarnated blockages. They could be from our parents, our teachers, our pastors, or our scout leaders. They could be from the reigning culture. They could be damning messages that were imprinted into our souls. They could come from some past failure that shamed us into collapse. They could be from some subtle or not so subtle message that our peers put upon us and which we wore as an invisible cloak of shame and fear all our lives … "You're a … , your *whatever* is too big, too small, too long, too short."

So often we are inhibited from living our own *greatness* because others made us feel small, wrong, insignificant and impoverished.

It is a huge mission for most of us to let go of these infra/extra structures that *inhabit* and *inhibit* our self. We are called upon throughout our human journey to let go of the past and to get on with life. Or stay stuck. If we are to embrace our own future, at last, it is important to get on with it and let the past be the past. Stop living and reliving past scripts that didn't work. We might call them "nostalgia lies."

In this last part of our life, one of the best gifts we can give to the next generation is to *understand* this slavery, to work at escaping from it and to pass on our newfound wisdom and radiance to them. Encourage them to dare the impossible. Help them acknowledge their dreams and deepest aspirations. Help them "work out" how they could possibly embrace their tomorrows with delight. Pain and despair do not produce healthy adults.

This encouragement is not done by keeping silent. It is done by conversation, time found with the next generation, by writing, by playing with them. It is done in the middle of playing a board game with grandchildren or in the middle of a car ride when there are only the two of you facing bravely ahead as you drive into the future.

My friend, Russell, called me aside when I visited our local general store a while back. He told me he wanted to show me some notes that he had come across, from a great aunt. They were very literary ramblings that this old woman made in order to preserve the story of her survival and that of her family as they pioneered in the Canadian West in the early twentieth century.

To have experienced the delight on his face as he read me page after page of this intriguing story, changed the energy of my day. He shared with me what courage he gained from the stories of the near-death escapes, the struggles with disease and the forces of weather and poverty in those days. What a heritage for him. What a thrill for me to be part of the saga that shaped our nation.

The fact that a woman from the middle of nowhere could describe the life that she lived with gusto and courage sends enormous energy into my life here and now. What a generous gift she left us—stories for our edification (i.e. our building up).

My little challenges pale beside the heroic things she had to do, day after day, in order to survive. She was able to put life into context. In writing these notes to her nieces and nephews, she was, indeed a beloved elder — even for me, a stranger.

An old friend

After the unfortunate visit with my friend in Zagreb in the late 1970s, as I recounted earlier, I left with a new friend I had never dreamed I would encounter: Nikos Kazantzakis. The one I had planned to encounter stood me up. The one I found would be more faithful and had much more staying power. Even though he was dead, he became an elder to me. A wise old man with many, many stories.

Like everybody's story, his story is compelling. He spins magic with words and images to describe his journeys through life. His language clarifies the chaos with which I sometimes find myself living. It is always a gift for me to find myself on his pages.

Every year, during Lent, I begin to read about his journey through life. He takes me places I have often refused to go. He ventures into territories that, in the end, liberate me and give me wings to fly. I notice, from my annual notes in the margins of his book, that I have birthed new thoughts and dreamed new dreams every year. I noticed that I had written in the margins, musical suggestions to listen to each year.

The sounds, the words, the atmosphere surrounding this sacred Lenten activity, have taken me to a place I long for, a place I seldom have the courage or the grace to embrace. I become one with my present, past and future and am granted the courage to *be*.

I picked up this precious volume — now well tattered — on Ash Wednesday last year, and noted that, inside the front cover I had two inscriptions:

> I began this Aeneid in Zagreb, in the desert, early September, 1979
>
> And again
>
> I continued in another andropausal pit in July 1998 — on the eve of a New Jerusalem.

I began to wonder about the 1998 *andropausal pit.* At the time, we were living in Parkdale, in the heart of Toronto. We were in the midst of building Ash Croft, our home in the country. I was in one of those in-between pits. I knew that what we were creating would be wonderful. We had designed it ourselves. It was a dream. Yet I was sad. I was anxious, on one hand, to leave the city, its noise, heat and dirt.

On the other hand, I was afraid of the unknown. That ranged from expenses to isolation. I was down.

I had picked up the writings of Kazantzakis, hoping to find some solace. I often did. He had become a friend to measure my days and nights against. Kazantzakis' *Report to Greco* has been that for me.

Is there some similar writing that captures your imagination: sacred scriptures from your religious tradition, poetry, a biography, a journal or a novel, a favourite author? Why not set them apart in your home, on some shelf where only very precious things are put? Or in a quiet room that gathers your "sacred" treasures — the ones that inspire or support your living. Why not reserve certain readings, music or art for particular times of the year, or for particular moods?

Or, it might be a season that plays that role in your life. I am always grateful for the liturgical seasons that my particular faith's tradition proposes each year. These festivals offer possibilities for reconstruction and re-alignment in my life. The recurrence of Easter, which we celebrate with great fires, processions, foods, songs and dancing at Ash Croft, leads me through the deaths and resurrections that each new year brings. Rituals have great importance in my life venture.

I am sure you have times and seasons that mark your life: Ramadan, Pesach, Dawali, Lent. Each gives a new opportunity to reflect and readjust your life. To enter into mythical times and spaces can give you great courage to be. And to have something to measure up against, a recurring event or reading, can lead you home. The fact that such times occur annually, gives you a template upon which you can situate yourself each year.

Photographs and keepsakes

Most people have a drawer somewhere, or an old shoe box, filled with pictures of people and events that have long gone beforehand. So many people have told me about photos they found in their parents' homes after their deaths. Sometimes there are photos of unknown persons.

Such links to past times could be valuable to us in our own lives. Oftentimes, it is only after the death of one of our elders that we struggle to re-identify ourselves, and often, in those times of deep loss, we try to reconstruct our selves from threads of information from our past. In life, we often walk past our elders. Once we lose them, we attempt, in any way possible, to find significance that we didn't bother with while they were alive.

I have helped hundreds of people prepare eulogies for the funerals of their elders. It is often the first time a whole community of people attempts to find meaning in the life of the deceased. It is often at that time that the true work of *personal growth somewhere* begins.

More and more families put photographs around the funeral home, in order to remember the life lived by the deceased person. But it is also an attempt to manifest the lives of the people touched by that life.

People will often wander around the funeral home looking for photos of themselves with the deceased, hoping that some meaning can come to them from some past event they shared. Everyone wants to be "related to" the person who has died.

But, why wait until then? Why not begin *now* with the photos you have piled away somewhere? Why not begin *now* to put them into some sort of order? Why not print information on the backs of them to identify the faces and events?

My aunt and uncle did a wonderful thing for all of my cousins several years ago. They went through their photos and selected for each of us those photos that captured moments of our lives together. As we arrived at their apartment, we were greeted in the foyer by posters made up of our stories in picture. Each of us received an album a few weeks later, which my aunt and uncle had prepared as a gift for us. It didn't take much money, just some time and energy. My album included not only photos, but also letters I had sent them in my teens, sometimes very naïve and pious as I look back on them now. They were precious to them. They treasured them enough to save them all those years.

I have two aunts who have always known that I value family stories. Both my Aunt Florence in Detroit (now buried there) and my Aunt Marjorie in Toronto, welcomed me into the intimacy of their cedar chests and closets. It was a true adventure to travel the years with them through their buried treasures, to unearth the stories of survival, both tragic and victorious, that have been buried in such things as quilts, shawls, rosaries, rings, brooches, pocket watches, cuff links and other keepsakes.

They each wanted to give me something from their treasure chest to have on my person before they died, so that the stories would go on and on.

My Aunt Marjorie was engaged to Gordon in her late teens. They were not allowed to marry because she was Roman Catholic and he was Presbyterian. A *mixed marriage* was strictly forbidden in those days. There was, at least for the Catholic, pain of eternal damnation. For the Protestant, there was the pain of shunning for marrying outside that tribe. As a result, they both married others and lived happy lives with them. He married twice. Upon the death of his second wife, he sought out his first love. They were both in their eighties.

They were like kids. Together at last! And what a glorious gift it was for all the families. We had all come from the same small town and most of us had grown up side by side, so it was a new kind of reunion for many old friends, under this new umbrella of the love of our elders.

A few years ago, they joined us for Easter dinner. After dinner, Gordon took my Aunt into the kitchen where we have a quilt that was put together by my grandmother, likely in the 1920s. It is an amazing "log cabin" quilt, made up from fragments of life at that time: my grandfather's night shirt, my mother's dresses, bits and pieces of clothing from my aunts and uncles and anything else that fit into the colour scheme. It truly is a beautiful piece of abstract art.

Gordon took my Aunt by the hand and led her to the quilt. He said, "That fabric," he said to her, referring to a yellow plaid cotton, "is from the dress you were wearing the first time I remember laying eyes on you, when you were fourteen."

That story brings tears to the eyes of so many people, when they hear it told. That lovely old quilt carries the energy of the people whose clothing dances together in it. It is a precious gift! My grandmother would be so proud that it enhances our home and our imagination.

Legacy

Every time I wander along the miles of paths that criss-cross our country property, I say a prayer of gratitude to Dick Spurr. We bought the property from Dick and his wife Ruby in 1997. It was a section of land that they had purchased in the 1960s. The land was turning, little by little, to desert. The government offered people money to plant trees in order to stabilize the land and to restore the forest.

When Dick and Ruby decided to sell this piece of the total farm, they insisted that the buyer would have to be a very special type of person. They had many prospective buyers but few who could pass the *Dick Spurr test*.

Dick needed someone who could continue his legacy. He had invested incredible energy into the forest. He knew that planting trees was more than merely planting trees. He began a process of restoration that would ensure the return of vegetation that had been obliterated by farming. It would also provide a habitat for animals who no longer had a home here. It would better the quality of air in the region, as well as in the nearby cities. It would re-establish water sources — these are headwaters that supply the rivers flowing into Lake Ontario and Lake Simcoe — and the greening of the county would be assured. Dick's legacy was to put into place a life-support system that would ensure a better quality of life for humans, flora, birds and animals for generations to come. He chose us.

Dick gave us a book by Jean Giono, *The Man Who Planted Trees*. The book is about Elzéard Bouffier, who did the same thing in Provence, beginning in 1910. His work was a heritage bequeathed to future generations. It was done with quiet determination, without fanfare. It had tremendous value. What had become a wasteland in Provence, due to ignorance and human greed, was transformed. Bouffier's attentive care of the newly planted forest would benefit the community for generations. Where old communities had died out, new families came from far and wide to live lives that were fuller than before.

As I look at a city like Toronto, a huge international centre with millions of people, I appreciate more and more the legacy of the people who created its parks system. High Park is a beautiful oasis in the centre of city. Along with the numerous other parks that have been sculpted along the rivers, by the lake and in every neighbourhood throughout the city, it enhances the life of the citizens.

Someone had to imagine and create them. Was it just a benefit of money left by generous donors to the city? Not at all. These forests are the lifeline of our communities. Not only do they purify the air for us, provide cool havens for our leisure, they also create gathering places for the thousands of people who live in apartments and have no green space of their own. How invigorating to see the latest immigrants enjoying their new-found land — eating, singing, dancing, doing Tai Chi, and playing in these neighbourhood havens.

Some people in our community have recently bequeathed land to the government as a heritage to the future — land that is to remain parkland in perpetuity. What gracious gifts these elders have bestowed.

Wealthy city developers have attempted to create a golf course and hundreds of homes on a hundred-acre parcel of land nearby. They also wanted to create an amphitheatre and all the supporting buildings to accommodate outdoor concerts and other events, mainly for cottagers who stop by on their way north to the lakes. The ecological consequences were going to be costly. The sound and light pollution would have been horrendous. The water required to support golf courses, the pesticides used to keep the greens weed-free — all would have had harmful effects on the humans, the wildlife and the future of the earth.

We have, in the surrounding area, a few groups made up of mainly seniors, who work valiantly for the good of future generations. These people do everything they can to ensure health for our communities and for the future of the earth through their vigilance and advocacy.

These local groups went after the developers. They had public meetings, gathered money, obtained signatures and raised consciousness in the community and throughout the province. They are winning.

There have also been attempts by some "land owners" in our rural community to bottle and sell the water on their land. They bought the land and so they felt they could do with it as they please.

What they forgot was that the water source came from underground lakes and rivers that provide water for many of us in the area. Those aquifers support the ecosystem that has formed above and below them. To deplete these underground aquifers is to steal from the community as well as from the future inhabitants of the land. There has, to this point, been no legislation to protect us from such ventures. Concerned community groups have been working relentlessly to save our precious water system.

After hundreds of gatherings, surveys and petitions, they were able to convince the government that the current legislation was not adequate to protect the environment from abuse by a few greedy residents. They have fought hard to protect these waters and the life that depends on them. They are winning once again.

These are men and women who have taken their responsibility seriously as elders in the community and have stopped "progress" so that we all might progress in health.

It is interesting that these same individuals also seem to be concerned about the arts in the community. There is a solid link between the two — the earth and the imagination.

Our local Arts Council is also a group made up, for the most part, of people over fifty. They ensure that the arts are celebrated in our communities. Concerts, art showings, talks and theatre all happen in this rural haven because of the work of these people.

Perhaps their greatest contribution is in their support for the arts among the youngsters. Art scholarships are created. Young people are rewarded for their work. Their art, music and writings are celebrated with those of the adults in all the shows. They are provided with means to explore their talents.

This group supports the schools as well as after-hours programs and treasures what our kids bring to the community. They invite the mature artists in the area to teach the young, to get to know them personally and to encourage them. This is true eldering.

For many years, there was a wonderful old man who wandered around the county and, without any permission, installed houses for bluebirds. No one ever saw him do it. The birdhouses just appeared! The bluebird had disappeared from our landscape. It has now returned. Sheldon Anderson recently died, but his legacy lives on. In fact, I received a bluebird house for a birthday present from a friend, who is making them now. I have learned that there is a group of Sheldon's disciples who carry on his work in secret!

Meaningfulness

The streaming began when we were little kids. IQ tests put us into groupings of smart, awfully smart and not smart at all. It was always surprising to me that I would be classified in the top batch of kids. I went to a private school and was in the scholarship class. I was always in the top five or so of my class — often the first. Yet, I believed I was stupid and a sham. I never really liked what we had to learn in school. I disliked the regimentation, the learning by rote, the atmosphere of shaming and the lack of official fun (of course, we made our own).

There were aspects of my being that never were accessed in the school system. In fact, I only ever met one or two professors, one in undergraduate and one in graduate school, who had any clue as to who I might be. My piano teacher knew who I was, although he only taught me Bach and Beethoven — never Kelly. Later, in the Dominican Order, I began to encounter more meaning and people who recognized who I was. Generally, I was bored. I had few good professors. Many of them were eminent men and world-renowned. But they were boring in the classroom. I was able to get A's in most of my classes, but I was not very interested, likely because my being was never engaged. I never used my truest being and no one seemed very interested in helping my truest self come to birth.

It has been only in these past-midlife years that I have been able to *learn* with all my being. Only in these years have I been able to really access *my* library, *my* body, *my* soul and *my* muses. I *did* all the right things up to this point, but without my whole being. The IQ tests, the lectures and the learning that were offered honoured only one aspect of my being: reason.

Imagination, art, sexuality, spirituality, sensuousness were deemed to have so little to do with my value, and nothing to do with learning. They were not measurable and therefore of little use in the eyes of many of my elders. However, it was because of those very things that I became popular as a young man and sought after as a mature man. As it was in my learning, so it might have been in my living had I not dared to live outside the box. There was knowledge, but no soul. There was data, but no spirit.

This last gift of time grants us an opportunity to integrate the knowledge we have received and to translate it into our *own* language. I notice that more and more I am able to create my own syntheses. I am able to speak in my languages without footnotes from somebody else. I am able to have opinions *out loud* that can have some influence in the community. I can effect change by using all my being to speak truths. At long last, I can become and be known as poet, prophet and troubadour — myself. It is energy from my truest source that I can pass on to the next generation.

I have always wanted to read the books I have bought over the years. Why was I attracted to this one or that? Why did I carry this particular book across continents? For most of my life books were an extension of my ego, lined up on my shelves, and served as proof to the world that I was, indeed, someone. Many are in Latin, French, Spanish or Italian — proof that I truly am smart. That, perhaps, is all true. But I didn't actually believe it. They served as a mask, a pseudo-self that enhanced my poor little shamed lad.

Now, at this stage of my life, they are much more than that. I now know that I acquired them for deeper reasons. This book or that, this CD or that, grabbed my imagination and offered to open up new and intriguing doors for me. Now, at long last, I am starting to open those doors. I am reading things that I can integrate into my fuller synthesis as I pursue my dream of effectively enfleshing my great work for the world.

At last, I am able to see the deep meaning of my existence. I can embrace with great joy the mystery of my being and can live and die in peace.

I find that it is in the *movement* that comes with walks where my mind seems most to connect the synapses. It is then that I seem to be able to "get" the meaning of moments in my life. Events from the past whirl into the present and slip ever so tactfully into my consciousness. It is as though they are crying out to be assessed and filed somewhere. It is when my mind is not focused on some specific task that the knitting seems to take place. Perhaps it is going on all the time, but it awakens in me during this stillness.

Some of the events are wonderful and fill my heart with joy. But often, they are scenes from a palette of which I am not too proud. They are events I had stored away or had attempted to delete from my screen of consciousness. But they emerge, fresh as the day they were born and haunt my waking hours.

They define me, as much as do the actual events that I am sure have fashioned my being. They are often the spice in the stew, the tang that has made me *interesting*, or even more, has made me human. It is this dance between the appropriate and inappropriate, virtue and sin, ecstasy and agony, which gives life to the grace of existence. To forget that each of us is virgin *and* whore, is to forget the essence of our daily struggle for life.

Great work

It is likely a sign of aging. I find myself often looking through the obituaries when I pick up a newspaper. Sometimes I get involved in the lives of the people who have died. I wonder who they really were, what they meant to people, what kind of living they did while they were here.

I am aware of where they came from, what era they were born in, and who they leave behind. I often wonder what they *truly* left behind for the world. So much of most people's lives, these days, is about working at a job. Many die *on* the job. Many more die *from* the job. In the end, in the obituaries, it is seldom the job that is mentioned.

What about that work — the part of our life that has captured most of our energy? For most of our life, we were either enraptured or enslaved by our work. Initially, we embraced a "job" as a way to make money in order to support our daily living and that of our family. That activity allowed us to be responsible for our physical needs.

The bigger question is about "work." Did the job fulfill our deepest needs? Work is about energy that we exert, which manifests our soul. A *job* doesn't always do that. Often the job we embraced, or as some would say, *got stuck in*, was not in harmony with our soul and was simply *put up with.*

If that is where you have spent the bulk of your years, you might want to *realign*, or perhaps *align*, yourself with your soul. Maybe all those years of work robbed you of your soul. In that case, these final years of your life could offer you invaluable opportunities for enjoying satisfying activity that comes, not from outside you, but that is an honest manifestation of what your personal energy is all about. The dance between who you are and what you do is enormously challenging. It could fill your last years with joy that you have never before known. You could begin to explore and enjoy your *great work*, which will surely be remembered and appreciated by those who will follow you.

Your obituary, then, might be much more interesting because it will talk about the influence you had in your time. Some are fortunate enough to marry their great work and their job. Perhaps there is still time left for you.

Art

My friend Ron arrived at our front door a short while ago with a gift. It was an oil painting done by a Canadian woman, Enola Sutherland, around 1910. It is now hanging in our great room, along with many other wonderful pieces of art painted by various other artists. But there is something very special about this work and it enlivens our walls. It has the flavour of a time past. It has the energy of a woman who went outside the boundaries of her era and began to paint with the same vitality with which Emily Carr and the Group of Seven painted in Canada. She was able to plug into the excitement of the time and send it into the twenty-first century with great freshness. She was not a well-known artist, but she did leave a huge collection of her own work, capturing an epoch that we can all now embrace.

My grandfather, John F. Schuett, was also an artist. As a young man he painted wagons and decorated the doors of Bruce County homes with scenes from the area. Our family has only a few pieces of his work because the wagons and doors have gone the way of all flesh. His paintings reflect an energy that was sensitive, strong and very romantic. I knew my grandfather as a furniture store owner and a funeral director. The artist in him was unknown to me. However, it is the artist that lives with me now — both on my walls and in my enthusiasm as I paint. The greatest legacy from him is in the fervour I breathe as I look at his work.

One of his paintings that we have is of a farmer in a white smock and brown hat, playing a flute beside a barn. His dog is by his side, along with a flock of geese, and they are obviously enjoying his music. There is a horse looking over the doorway, and all the creatures seem to be involved in the music. Why did he paint these things? What did they represent to him? What was he like?

Like my grandmother's quilt, which hangs on our kitchen wall, these pieces are treasures that are priceless because they link us — not only to the past, but to the creative flair that exploded as these people went into the imaginary and experienced the universal phenomenon that we sometimes call the divine. They are very strong links to what lies beyond and within.

In an historical time when we seem to want to fill our spaces with art and furniture that is modular, with contemporary lines, I am always impressed how some people crave for something from their family's past to serve as a link. Even things from the 1950s are creeping into contemporary homes. We seem to need these links. Perhaps we need the stability that the past affords us. Imagined stability. We are not alone. We are part of everything that preceded us.

As my aunts prepare to die, they seem very happy to give me gifts from their treasure chests. I know how difficult it must be for them to part with things that have helped define them in their lives. Silverware, dishes, linens — things that they seldom use any more — lovely things that punctuated lovely lives lived in the past.

The recipes are also part of that treasure chest. Surely the art of cooking was every bit as essential to the energy of the creative spirits who preceded me. Desserts seem to rule in our family. There are no recipes of savoury foods passed on — other than sauerkraut (*choucroute*), which came through the Alsatian connection. I wish I had the crocks that I remember the cabbage slept in during the winter months.

How often the taste or the look of a particular food can take us back to the experiences we had when eating them with our elders. Food holds memory. Scents hold memory. All of this is part of the artistic stretch towards the fullness of being human.

In our family, we have an elaborately embroidered, long white gown that we all wore at our baptism. It has been worn since the early 1900's. Each new child born into our family wears it. It is a strong sacrament of the energy of faith that generations have embraced.

I have always thought that it would be a good tradition to create a family funeral pall (a large cloth blanket), which would be used in a family to cover the casket at each funeral. In the church it is used to represent the white gown of baptism and is placed on the casket as it arrives at the church for the funeral. In these days when so many families have no ties to faith communities, it might serve well as a link between generations and could serve as a "comfort-er" in the dance of saying goodbye to the departed.

I met a widow a short time ago, who told me that she had experienced a terrible struggle as she attempted to clean out her husband's closet after his death. In a streak of genius, she decided to carefully deconstruct his clothing and weave the fabric into the form of old

Quebec rag-rugs. She has created throws for herself, her children and for her husband's mother. What a creative way to pass on energy, memories and deep comfort.

I always love visiting friends who are delighted to share stories around heritage pieces that they have embraced after someone has died. They inevitably enlighten me about my friends. Through the pieces I always discover new contours, new zest, new hues about my friends. They are often keys to the hidden history — name changes, religion changes, country changes — that were the prelude to life in this country. Very often they magnify the kind of courage or integrity that my friends have inherited. The pictures, art pieces, cutlery or dinnerware represent a vivid tapestry that helped create the human I stand before.

The people are the true works of art. These pieces grace them.

Prophetic voices

The major prophets of this era have come out of many places.

Now and again there has been an Archbishop Tutu or Archbishop Ted Scott, of the Anglican churches in South Africa and Canada. They were strong men, whose voices echoed loudly through the valleys of darkness. We expect prophetic gestures from religious leaders — although, too often they find themselves embedded with the powerful oppressors of the poor.

Still others have emerged from the cracks of our society and have used the gifts of age and wisdom to the betterment of the human race and the earth. Everyone is a mystic, and all men and women have the seeds of wisdom. The gift of prophecy is a gift that is often neglected even though it is innate. Every human has a voice for survival. Some have developed it. Some just need to discover or uncover it.

Jane Jacobs is a strong, prophetic voice from the city of Toronto. She has been an enthusiastic advocate for healthy cities and, as a visionary, has proclaimed the five pillars of society necessary to "stand firm."

They are community and family, higher education, the effective practice of science and technology, self-policing by the professions and the application of taxes and other government powers to society's needs and possibilities.

Jacobs has been ferocious in her fight to bring political forces in line with human needs. In these latter days, she has sent strong warnings out to our governments.

> The world today is a bewildering mosaic of cultural windows, groups of people sunk into old or recent dark ages and downward spirals, groups in the process of climbing out, and remnants of pre-agrarian cultures, as well as

> remnants of declining empires. Even within cultures, mosaics and modern, ancient and dark-age cultures exist.

And she continues in *Dark Age Ahead: Caution:*

> Some people think optimistically that, if things get bad enough, they will get better because of the reaction of beneficent pendulum swings …
>
> Corrective stabilization is one of the great services of democracy, with its feedback to rulers from the protesting and voting public … But powerful persons and groups that find it in their interest to prevent adaptive corrections have many ways of thwarting self-organizing stabilizers.

Governments fear people like Jane Jacobs. Her presence demands truth telling. Her wisdom is notorious and her track record for justice is a sword to contend with. She has a voice that is even stronger because she is "just an old woman."

Audrey Shenandoah is a clan mother of the Onondaga Nation of North American First Nations Peoples. She says that a clan mother is chosen by people watching how she lives her life and how she cares for her family.

> She has to be someone who has a family and knows the responsibilities of being a mother, because that's evidence that she will take care of all the people as if they were her own children.

In native circles, the clan mothers are the ones who choose (and dethrone) the chiefs. Their wisdom is magnified by their gathering together in the clan circle.

Shenandoah's reflections on the clan mothers led me to think of the Raging Grannies, who have been a strong voice for justice across our nation. Their comical costumes, witty songs and persistence have made many a government shudder at their presence. Age is their strongest credential. They have been there.

Age can be a very powerful tool. Too old can be even stronger.

In the 1970s the Vatican struck up a commission to study the question of the ordination of women within the Roman Catholic Communion. The results hinged radically upon the investigations into the scriptures of the Christian Bible. After several years of study, the biblical team announced to Pope Paul VI that there was *no biblical evidence* for or against the ordination of women to the ministry of presbyterate. In the final declaration, however, the Pope proclaimed officially that there was evidence in the scriptures to make it clear that women could not be ordained.

Father David Stanley was a brave and prophetic Jesuit from the Toronto Province of the Society of Jesus. He was well into his seventies when, in an article in *The Globe and Mail* that same week, he asserted that the Vatican had lied. Period. The research said one thing. The Pope said another. A lie. Period.

At a conference where we both addressed the major superiors of religious orders in Canada, I thanked him for his courage. He looked at me — at that time the youngest Prior in the Order of Preachers — and he smiled and said: "I'm old enough to tell the truth now. I'm too old for them to hurt me." What a freedom!

Pauline Vanier was the wife of our former Governor General, Georges Vanier, who served this country with dignity and grace in the 1960s. Georges Vanier died in 1967. Pauline died in 1991 at the age of ninety-two.

Mme Vanier had *adopted* me as another son and upon the death of the Governor General asked that I spend time with her at Government House. She was in deepest grief. My superior at the time forbade me to go, telling me that we were meant to serve the disenfranchised and the poor. In a very strong and deliberate voice — I was twenty-four — I told him that if the vice-regent of the Queen had asked for me to be with her for a few days, for some music and comforting conversation, I would have to disobey him in honour of a higher imperative. She was, because of her grief, both poor and disenfranchised. I disobeyed him. I went.

It was clear to me that even if Pauline Vanier was "just" the wife of the Governor General, she was much more to the nation. She was the strong spiritual source of life for her husband and for her children. In many ways she was the "mother" of Canada.

In her time remaining at Government House, Mme Vanier acted as head of state. At her seventieth birthday, surrounded by all the foreign ambassadors, this woman was hailed as the "chief." Her beauty and wisdom had captured the hearts of the nation and of the nations. Her greatest gift to me and to thousands was that of her strong, gracious and holy *presence.* She did not have to say a word. She had become an icon for the nation.

In the years after her time in Ottawa, she joined her son, Jean, the venerable founder of *l'Arche*, in France. There she spent the remainder of her life living in community with handicapped adults in the community at Trosly. She did not have to do that. She chose it. Her presence was prophetic. After that there was never a public word spoken. *But she was there. Prophet.*

Many times, we think that to be prophetic requires a loud voice. My mother, Lucille Lettner, was a quiet, unassuming "housewife." She died at forty-nine. It was only at the visitation in the funeral home where I discovered that my quiet, gentle mother was a much revered and respected member of a community. I was unaware that she had influenced many. Women approached me to tell me how funny my mum was, how they had wanted to elect her president of the Catholic Women's League but how she always refused because she was afraid to speak publicly. She did not speak with words, but she did speak with humour, a smile and compassion. Prophecy is consistent with each personality.

Discover *your* voice.

Bruce Gray is an actor friend of ours who lives between Hollywood and Toronto. He has enjoyed a successful career on stage, screen and television. He has more time available to him these days than he did in his youth, and has decided that, at this period of his life, he will pass on the art of acting to the next generation.

The neighbourhood public school is the launching pad for this great adventure. No sounding trumpets. Just kids. It has been an instrument for tremendous breakthrough in the community. Acting allows the children to speak words that they could not speak on their own steam, to dream dreams that are bigger than their neighbourhood or family allows. It also encourages them to stretch in ways they could never imagine. All this is made possible through the generous gift of an aging man who wants to leave something from his great work to the newcomers. Generous, gracious and full of stories!

♪♪♪

Although we often cringe with the thought of growing old, there is reason to delight in the idea, as well. There is a great gift to be offered to the future generations, if we make a concerted effort to be old. With age comes wisdom. With age come stories and with age comes a savouring that cannot be known in our youth. We must not masquerade as youth. Not only is it not attractive, but it does not answer anyone's true need. The young need older adults to be beside them, to listen to them, to question them, to cry with them and to dance with them.

♪♪♪

What stories that were passed down to you remain with you to this day? Did those who journeyed before you have sayings, phrases, prayers or stories that you want to hang on to? Were there stories of escape from a foreign land? Stories of survival during tough times? Stories of the birth of your parents, of yourself? Were there strong gestures or warnings about the times we live in? About the times they lived in? Were there prophetic statements that can apply to your life today?

What kinds of *flashes* do you have of their energy? Of their humour? Of their holiness or wholesomeness? Are there attitudes that you have embraced because of flashes of them that accompany you on your journey through life? I have images of my elders that remain in my mind and heart, which are grander than photos or items from them. It is as if that energy translates into my life as a fresh story told in a new era. It's strange, how they remain with us.

What are some of the stories, gestures, attitudes and wisdom that you feel you should or want to pass on to the next generation? Are there things that could help save them, that could enhance their lives, strengthen their journey? Are there beliefs that you have inherited, or that you have espoused for your own health and salvation, which could be of benefit to them?

Don't worry. The next generation has innate wisdom to carry them through the world they will live in. But are there signs of the times that you, with your older wisdom, might want to point out to them? You do not need to give them answers. But you might want to indicate or suggest questions they might ask. You might see trends returning again that should be highlighted. Don't forget, with your death, goes a wealth of experience.

Listen to Jane Jacobs, once again:

> A couple of decades ago, it was common to hear residents remark … that they never used to need to lock their doors. Nowadays, the remark is seldom heard. People who once didn't need to lock their doors have gradually died off, and so, even the memory of what has been lost, is now almost lost.

We could learn a great deal about shared wisdom from the old Sufi story of the melon hunter.

> Once upon a time, there was a man who strayed from his own country into the world known as the Land of Fools. He soon saw a number of people flying in terror from a field where they had been trying to reap wheat.
>
> "There is a monster in that field," they told him. He looked, and saw that it was a watermelon.
>
> He offered to kill the "monster" for them. When he had cut the melon from its stalk, he took a slice and began to eat it. The people became even more terrified of him than they had been of the melon. They drove him away

> with pitchforks, crying, "He will kill us next, unless we get rid of him."
>
> It so happened that at another time another man also strayed into the Land of the Fools, and the same thing started to happen to him. But, instead of offering to help them with the "monster," he agreed with them that it must be dangerous, and by tiptoeing away from it with them he gained their confidence. He spent a long time with them in their houses until he could teach them, little by little, the basic facts which would enable them not only to lose their fear of melons, but even to cultivate them themselves.

It is imperative that we, as elders in the community, proclaim hope for tomorrow. That grows from a deep sense that we have been able to live valuable lives in our time. How are we to be prophetic and read the signs of our time? It is, indeed, by living until the final moment that we will be the wisdom that the next generation deserves. Be visible. Be heard. Be the gift that you are for the world. Do not hide under any bushel basket.

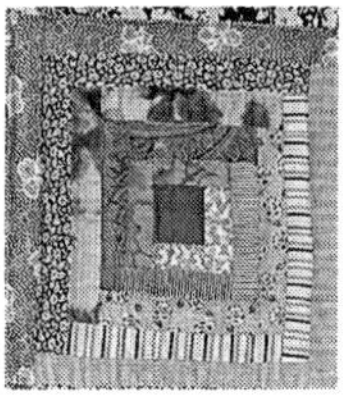

5

Leaving Home: The Process of Growing up and Finally Embracing Death

I work all day. And get half drunk at night
Waking at four to soundless dark, I stare.
In time the curtain edges will grow light.
Till then I see what's really always there
Unresting death, a whole day nearer now,
Making all thoughts impossible but how
And where and when I shall myself die.
Arid interrogation; yet the dread of dying, and being dead,
Flashes afresh to hold and horrify.
And so it stays just on the edge of vision
A small unfocused blur, a standing chill
That slows each impulse down to indecision
Most things may never happen; this one will.

— *Aubade, Philip Larkin*

Facing death

I've lived and died a thousand times. Sometimes they were huge deaths and at other times, small. They ranged from loss of teeth as a child (with obvious rewards) to loss of hair as a young man, to loss of friendship, partnership and community. They all preface what I feel is the ultimate death.

For so many years of my life I was the youngest of everything. I poised myself to be young. That has changed. Now I am the oldest in the group of friends we hang out with. I don't feel or act the oldest, but indeed, I am.

Last week I was at the funeral of another friend — younger than I am. As I sat in the church awaiting the arrival of my friend's body in a casket, I began to remember all those my age and younger who are no longer with us in body. They are becoming legion. It started when I was a boy, with the death of a few schoolmates. But as the years go on, there seem to be more of us *there* than *here*. I know, from my experiences with the elders in my life that they often feel alone, as they become the last child in the family, or the last of their friends, or the survivor of a second or third marriage.

I am beginning to have dreams about the dead. The players come alive again, generally younger than they were when they died. But they come to me. They talk to me, encourage me, laugh with me. Are they preparing me to join them? Where is this going? One of my elderly aunts awakens in the night to the voices of her sisters. She goes to the bathroom and tries not to disturb my mum who is asleep in the bed beside her (my mum has been dead since 1962). Where does the line begin and end between these two horizons — the here and now and the hereafter? As we age, does it diminish and become a dotted line? I believe so.

While I have always had a fear of death, I am becoming acutely aware of its inevitability. I confront it and try to turn what has been abhorrent to me into a positive moment. Major shifts in my life were always overwhelmingly fear-filled. But I took the road and breathed my way into what I had envisaged would be a horrible moment. I never died from any of it.

There is no way around this one. I cannot control it. It is inevitable and there is nothing that I can do to prevent it. It is inscribed into the nature of humankind, of *earth-creatureliness*. So why not allow myself to let go and venture into the unknown? I've done it before.

Death could be a most positive journey. I have always tried to believe it is so. I have always gathered from the various religious traditions — including my own — that there is hope for a next moment. I have always preached it. Was it to convince myself? Is there something innate that we just *know* about?

Ivan Illich, one of my old heroes, a man who influenced my life and work enormously, a man who taught me to live life fully and on the edge when I lived with him in Cuernavaca in the sixties, spoke about this before he died in 2002.

> Yes, we suffer pain, we become ill, we die. But we also hope, laugh, celebrate: we know the joy of caring for one another; often we are healed and we recover by many means. We do not have to pursue the flattening-out of human experience. I invite all to shift their gaze, their thoughts, from worrying about health care to cultivating the art of living. And today, with equal importance, the art of suffering, the art of dying.

Consummate your life

As I witness people preparing for death, I am struck by the fact that so many of them seem to embrace life with a new-found fervour. They embrace life uncompromisingly. It is important that we not spend enormous energy fighting death. We cannot escape death.

What a gift to yourself, and to all involved in your life, if you use your good energy to embrace living. As you approach death, the terror of the unknown might captivate your energy. Deal with the issues surrounding *your* death and, if need be, get help to do it well. Concentrate on living. Consummate your life!

Have you lived your life, or been lived *by* it? You might have *achieved* a great deal — wealth, importance, family and children — but regardless of what you have achieved, have *you* been the one living your life? Have you chosen it? Have you lived your life or lived the life assigned you?

It takes a great deal of courage and encouragement to exit the trap of unenlightened living. Our Western economic and even our spiritual systems can entrap us in a mindset that makes it very difficult for us to *live life* rather than to be *lived by* our lives. It requires a healthy stance *vis-à-vis* not only the "divine" (however you define that), but also the material and social. It requires a freedom to choose a lifestyle that *you* own, the freedom to shape the final years of your life *any which way you choose.*

That could mean the possibility of leaving or entering a relationship, a country, ways of socializing, ways of practicing belief, ways of working or not. This is a very serious matter. There is no better time than now to embrace your life.

We have work to do if we are to embrace death. I have seen so many people *die* before they died, because they gave up the right to fashion their lives. I have seen people die because they did not have the courage, strength or environment necessary to claim *their own lives.* And I have seen even more people who died caught in the web of propriety, social acceptance or religious tyranny.

This is a time for radical truth-telling. The support of an elder or a group can be so helpful at this time of life. Many of the pivotal choices I have made in my life — *for life* — were encouraged by gracious *mid-wives* who knew me and my deepest aspirations and encouraged me to "go" or to "let go."

Often, these choices are not understood by those

who have surrounded us most of our lives, since they themselves established the traps we were caught in. Perhaps they are so embedded in them personally that they find it hard to understand the choices for integrity that we might dream of embracing.

It is never too late. The choices we make, at this stage of life, could serve us well. They could also be a great support to others, and give them courage to dance their own dance.

Gerry Judd is an old man now. In his eighties, he is still a beacon of light for many. He would not be offended to be called an "old man." In his younger years, like so many of us in our generation, he became a minister in the church. After serving as pastor for some time, he became part of the leadership of his denomination.

After seventeen years of marriage, his wife drowned and left him to raise three little children. That likely triggered what followed.

Gerry began a new adventure. In his personal life and in his ministry, he began to see a *disconnection* between the spirit and the body, between spirituality and sexuality. He began a long exploration that took him from Esalen to Alexander Lowen and from Christianity to other *approaches* for spiritual growth. This new synthesis continued to grow as he began to explore the roots of the divide. He saw that people were not stuck in their conscious minds but in a deeper level, which he calls the "Twilight Zone."

His work, first with clergy and their partners and then with larger groups, led him to explore this deeper level of *stuckedness* and to find ways of transforming it. He established a centre called *Shalom Mountain* in the Catskills, in New York State, where he could work with individuals and groups. He turned his sadness into a gift for many.

As he grew into his late seventies, he decided that *he* needed to deal with his own last times and to help others deal with the ultimate questions of life and death. So he founded *Timshel*, a new centre in a new place, in Pennsylvania. It offers people an arena for dealing with the ultimate *disconnection* we often feel between our spirit and our body — between this life and the next.

Gerry Judd has *lived* his life, *loved* his life and *consummated* his life.

For him, death has no sting. His great work has been to help people take the leaps required for *true living* at every crucial stage of their life. Now, because of his imaginative adventure, many are able to embrace their dying as well as their living.

Lots of Time

> Idleness … does not consist in doing nothing but in doing a great deal not recognized in the

dogmatic formularies of the ruling class … Extreme busyness … is a symptom of deficient vitality.

— *Robert Louis Stevenson*

I have discovered that all human evil comes from this, man's being unable to sit still in a room.

— *Blaise Pascal*

There is a heresy in modern living that canonizes activity. To think that these sages from times past could write such words, shows me that there must be something inherent in humankind that dislikes vacuum. Generally we fill those spaces with sound, stuff, busyness. It is not uncommon to find "retired" people busier after their retirement than they ever were while they "worked." Many of them brag about it. Many of them die from it. Elders suffer burnout in amazing numbers. Many deplete their immune systems with frantic activity. Some, on the other hand, wade into old age with sense and sensitivity.

The last time I saw my beloved Uncle Godfrey, he was holding court in the village restaurant in his little town.

He was surrounded at one table by his wife, her sisters and a variety of their granddaughters. He was dressed in his usual shirt, natty tie and beautiful blue suit. He would encourage them to have pie to end the noon meal and he would insist on looking after the bill. He was a very generous man. He always took time to eat. He took time to chat, time to linger with people.

He died on the eve of his eighty-seventh birthday.

The week before his death he decided to buy a new suit. He had lots of suits but, since he went to work every day until the day he died, he felt that he needed to look good and a new suit was always in order. He always looked good. I can't remember ever seeing him without a shirt and tie (even at the beach). He was buried in the new suit.

Close to a thousand people came to his wake. In a village, which was barely that large, it took a great man to bring so many people together. They talked about how he knew them. He cared about them. Even the children were worthy of a conversation with Godfrey. Nobody was too small or too poor to merit a story and some time. As I watched people gather at the funeral home, it was obvious that this little man had taken a great deal of time to affect people's lives. Many of them had tears in their eyes. Their "elder" was gone. Parish priests came and went, but Godfrey was the true pastor in the community. His furniture store was his stage and his ministry overflowed to thousands of hearts. He was the best known funeral director in the county. He took time, gave time and lost time well. He *lived his life*. He didn't let his life *live him.*

I sometimes live through a day and realize that I have done little. In fact, often I find myself waiting for the weekend, hoping that the days will scurry by in order to get me to Friday night. Then I grab myself by the collar with the reminder that, unlike when I was eighteen, I have only so many days left. I must value the time that is given to me. Every moment counts.

When I was young, the expression "time is money" was supposed to mean something to me. Now, I believe the expression "time is precious" to be more valuable. Time is the currency of life at this point. "Having" can become less important after mid-life. Time cannot be bought, bartered or traded.

I found myself on a cold November afternoon in the garden, cleaning up for the winter. The tubers from the dahlias and gladioli had to be collected for winter storage. My mind went, of course, to the winter.

I began to think about Christmases. How many are left? How many trees will we need to last us until we are no longer here? What will the last time be like? Will we know that it is the last time? Is it ten more, or fifteen, or twenty? Not likely twenty-five. Uncle Godfrey died at eighty-six, the longest living member of my family. When you start to count backwards rather than forwards, time takes on new value.

This season has a great deal to teach us about living and dying. We begin to prepare for a slower time — a time when the weather takes us by the hand and leads us into the unknown. It is impossible for us to control the weather in the months ahead. Snow can keep us indoors for days on end. Ice can isolate us. Cold and wind can stall us in our tracks. *We are not always in control.*

November is good for that kind of reflection. The falling of the leaves, the browning of the pastures, the dropping of the seeds — as we begin the long *darkening*, many of us naturally begin to think about death and the long winters that await us.

It also presents an opportunity to think about our need to take more time to do things. Take the extra time to get from one place to another. Take the time to dress properly for the winter. Take the time it takes to get outdoor chores done. Take quiet reflective time inside, in front of the fire, around the wood stove, over the soup pot on the stove, over a cup of tea.

This is a vital season for us to "incarnate" as we think about the cycle of life and death. As nature closes down for a rest, do the same. It is not a time of non-being. On the contrary, it is a time for recuperation, re-sourcing and for rebounding. None of this happens without first stopping.

Spring comes again after this long season of rest. And when it does burst forth into Passover and Easter, I am always mindful that the new life doesn't happen without the burial of the seeds, the falling of the leaves and the *deaths* that bring all of creation to a supposed stop.

Springtime always returns with hope of resurrection and new life. If it is so with all of the visible nature, why not with *our* nature?

Take Time

- To wake up in the morning. Reflect on the night past and the day ahead.
- To drink your coffee and sit for awhile.
- To have a bowel movement. Don't rush. Relax.
- To eat a good breakfast.
- To read something in the morning.
- To spend time with a few friends.
- To welcome visitors.
- To eat and savour your meals. You're not going anywhere.
- To just be. To contemplate and pray.
- To just sit.
- To walk and walk and walk as long as you can.
- To remember the past chapters of your life.
- To think about the future — even your dying and death.
- To go through old photograph albums.
- To write or phone old friends.
- Take time …

The tree

In our home, we begin the Christmas season in early December with the cutting of a great tree on our property. We chop off the top fourteen feet and haul it into the house. This is no small feat! It takes a tribe of us to cut it, pull it, wrap it, drag it, hoist it and, alas, decorate it! Every year we wonder at it. Wonder at ourselves. Also, we wonder why we bother with it at all! But most years we do bother and once it is done, we understand the reasons.

Once the tree is up and decorated, we celebrate it for the month and truly enjoy it. Our friends and family are enthralled with it every year.

Around the sixth of January, we are faced with the terrifying prospect of "taking down the tree." That involves storing the decorations carefully, winding up the strands of lights and chopping the branches off so we can easily take it to the place where we will eventually burn it.

As I take the decorations from the tree, I think of where each piece came from, the stories behind each one, the memories of friends who are with us still and friends who have departed this life. It is both sad and comforting.

That certainly makes me ponder my own journey. Once again, how much time is left? What am I doing with it? Have I lived up to my dreams, hopes, and commitments? How many "new starts" have I had along the way? How many did I follow through?

As I age, it becomes ever clearer to me that I have fewer chances to get things right. I had better bother to get them right the first time. That is a gift for me. Now is the hour.

The annual Christmas tree is a yardstick with which to measure my life. Thank heavens for rituals. They remind us of who we are and where we are on the journey. They bring friends together again, revitalize old memories and create new ones. They help us feel grace and bring solace to our days.

Signposts are important. Rituals that mark special times are as important for others as they are for ourselves. In an era where almost everything is secularized, people seem to scream out for events that create significance for them. Don't short-change these events. Meals could be memorable, visits could mark special times. Treasures that are pulled out once a year serve to underscore the significance of memorable days. Anniversaries and festivals can store up the memories that could keep many a winter warm.

A tree is not just a tree.

A band of elders

With the new year comes that dreaded word "resolution." As I began to think of it, I realized that this is a word that has accompanied me throughout my life. I made New Years' Resolutions for most of my life. I came across a list the other day from 1984 when I resolved to keep my desk tidy. To get to my desk by nine every morning. To keep my shoes shined. I still, this year, work on those little things.

As a child, going to confession in the Roman Catholic Church week after week, I "… firmly resolved to sin no more and avoid the near occasions of sin. Amen." I resolved, but it also included a helpful phrase, "… with the help of thy grace." Somehow that ancient wisdom understood that, on our own, we are pretty shaky. It takes the energy and care of another to bolster up that resolve.

Most of my attempts at integrity have been solo. In moments of enlightenment, however, I have chosen not to fly solo and have sought the presence of another to grace my journey. A companion sometimes can intervene in a direct manner and help with one's resolutions, or, by some hidden threads, support, remind, energize or threaten. At times, this companion has been a therapist; at times, a spiritual guru. At other times, a strong and compassionate friend. Sometimes it needed to be a woman, sometimes a man. Now and again, someone older. Sometimes the divine. The one thing that I have learned in my journey is that it is stupid to travel alone on this journey. It is not worth the pain and insecurity. The grace of another is such a simple yet wise idea.

Most of us are trying our best to live out these final years with sanity, wisdom and humour. I have often thought it would be a good idea to call together a band of elders who might share their wisdom and courage to help with major decisions for the journey.

Some of them might have one area of expertise, others another. You need to choose a healthy balance of individuals who exhibit "smart living."

You might decide to have a series of elders. Some for financial decisions, investment ideas, new projects for work or for living — buying, selling, moving, staying. Maybe some for new work orientations, retirement ideas, travel coaching. You might have some to help with life and death questions, personal issues.

I have a friend who discovered that he is terminally ill. He was frightened and alone. He pulled together a group of us who met every few months for a day and shared our energy with him. He and we were welcome to share whatever was important for the day. He felt great comfort that there were five other men who knew him and who would sustain him through the disease. That was ten years ago and he is fine. It could possibly be because of the energy, support, prayers and compassion of the group of friends.

There are more and more women gathering together, and when they do, they wear "red hats." Besides the fun of elegant, aging women gathering together, it creates a *constant* — a nineteenth century term to signify just that. Constancy is important in the years of vital decision making. So many of us have to make huge decisions about lifestyle — where to live, how to survive financially without a "job," to live alone or to risk living in a creative way with another person.

Constancy has great value in relationships. We can grow a great deal from a small group of people who know us to the core. We have a hard time keeping the truth from them. We also need the comfort and trust from these friends to be able to break down when necessary or break through when it happens. Such *midwives* can help us breathe and tell us when to push on.

Become the earth, the air, the sea and the skies

Contemplation is one of the simplest and most natural of all human activities. We are born with a contemplative nature and we are most at peace when we embrace that aspect of our lives. Everyone is a contemplative — not only monks. Contemplation is simply being one with everything that is in the stillness of the moment. It is to enter into the very mind of God.

Often, I decide to take the time and simply sit in the forest. In this primordial state, I little by little *become* the forest. It surrounds me. I am a part of the wind, the trees, the sounds and the earth. I can distance myself from all of this by thinking, or I can simply choose to be part of it. Time ceases, concerns fade and I *become* peace.

Humans in this epoch, distance themselves from the elementary. This is due to the kind of world we live in, which requires us to leave the natural world in favour of material prosperity. We have been carefully taught to gain the whole world to the detriment of our solitary peace. We tend to isolate ourselves from our core being, in honour of the *stuff-ing* that cushions our fall from grace.

We forget that we have gifts *and* limitations, that there are natural boundaries we cannot cross without becoming broken and sad. We need to re-root ourselves constantly in order to remain human. Otherwise, we lose our souls in honour of money and dubious security.

That re-rooting is not done with techniques and with programs. It only happens through emptying and quiet. It costs nothing, requires no props and needs no spiritual "school" to validate it. It is innate in us and is the most normal of our human activities — like breathing. Yet it feels foreign to most of us. Most of us avoid it in honour of being busy with things.

We cannot go into the uncharted (for us) waters of death with any peace at all if we have not tasted the core of our being in the quiet of the contemplative *moment*. We cannot leave "all of this" if we do not know the "that" into which we *flow* or *leap* when we die.

Sit or walk, and be still. That is all.

Let go

Much of our human identity comes from our "having." We are defined by what we do, where we live, where we come from, what we have achieved and who we have fostered. All that can be pretty compelling when what we are to embrace next seems like an entrance into the abyss. So, most people cling to those things "for dear life." Knowing we can't take them to the grave doesn't seem to help many.

Some even build monuments to themselves that will make their *stuff* contain their life. Some of the biggest monuments I have ever seen are about people who have become "no-bodies" because no one any longer has a clue as to who they were or what they were about. They might have done better to have put their energy into *letting go* and generously *giving away*, than to hanging on and on and on to their monuments.

Many people I know have given away items before their deaths. Some have given money. Some have given teacups. They are both important. Some have shared stories, or family secrets that help plough the fields for family truth-telling, healing and recovery. Some have kept life-long journals or written about their own life adventures in the autumn of their lives to leave to those left behind. What a great gift!

Some give the gift of love — tender, tangible and treasured — with the simple words, *I love you*.

I am very conscious that my dear aunt, as she ages, has made a point of using these sacred words every time she phones. She thus stays *with* me, as I face my own new tomorrows. So many of the living would have been redeemed with those simple words coming from the dad or mum or the sibling or mentor. And at what little cost!

I had dinner with that aunt recently. I did the cooking because she is having difficulty getting around. It was a little gesture for me but a huge one for her. She has always cooked magnificently and has been a beacon of generosity. Now it is my time to cook for her. I chose things I know she loves — things she can't readily afford — or, at least wouldn't allow herself to afford.

We partook of the meal and then the stories began. She reminded me that when she is gone, the stories will end. No one has the family knowledge that she does. As she talked, items that carried the stories began to appear — her silver serving dishes, which she received when she was married, photos of my ancestors, old letters. A world I had forgotten emerged. People came *in from the dark* through her stories and we laughed and cried.

At the end of the evening, she invited me to take the silver home. I will treasure the pieces. I will especially treasure the stories and the memories they carry.

Be prepared

"If you ever send me to one of those hellholes, I'll haunt you till you die." How many of us have heard those words addressed to us by some member of our family when faced with the prospect of a nursing home?

That was them. Next time, it might be you.

As we age, we would be smart to begin to prepare

for the next phase that awaits us. No one of us can design completely what that will be like. Most of us hope that death will conquer us as a thief in the night. We just won't wake up. But chances are we will have to face a long life, some of which will be spent doing little and somewhere other than at home.

Many of us live with a kind of hidden terror about what will happen to us when we will no longer be totally in control of ourselves. No class, gender, race or religion frees us from that reality. We fear being abandoned by those we trust will love us to the end. At times, we fear the treatment of the unknown caregivers.

Our life expectancy today has increased to the late seventies and eighties from mid-forties in 1900. In the next ten years, life is expected to extend, for one in twenty, to one hundred years. We can prepare or just wait and hide.

What can we do to prepare?

For one thing, think about it. In addition, plan to be comfortable with little. Begin to give things away. It is often when I travel, that I realize how little I can be happy with!

The nomadic existence should likely be our model. Who knows how often we will be required to move before the end of our lives?

Change things around now and again, even the furniture. Visit the elderly. Get to know what community living looks like and how it might look if *you* had anything to do with it. *Have something to do with it!* Now is a good time to get involved in elder care. Help change the system so that you will be assured the kind of care you would want when your time comes.

My Aunt Dorothy surprised me a few years ago when she announced that she was *going south*. I congratulated her — she was not at all an avid traveller. To do this in her eighties was a brave step. What she was planning to *do*, however, was an even braver step.

She was going 100 km south to visit a retirement home for the weekend! The facility's management had offered senior citizens the opportunity *to come see* and visit for the weekend. They made the price attractive. It included an opportunity for the guest to invite anyone of their choice to join them there for a meal as well. My aunt was courageous enough to take them up on their offer.

When I asked her how it went, she went on to tell me how delightful the experience was. "Two girls (both in their eighties) came to meet me upon my arrival. We had lunch, a rest and then … " She continued to regale me with tales of her stay. Cards, a glass of wine, fellowship, laughter.

She has graduated to a retirement home now, and moved west to be closer to her daughter, grandchildren and great-grandchildren. She now has a boyfriend from the home and is enjoying her last gift of time in ways she would never have imagined.

Why not put your name on a waiting list? Check out facilities that might please you — even if you are still in your sixties! Either set money aside for the day when you will need assisted living, or look into what your situation would be if you do not. At least know your options.

Talk about options for your future with your family and close friends. Take charge as much as you can. It is your life. You should decide how you want to live it, as much as you can.

Learn to occupy your time with things that you will be able to do later in life. Create a life beyond TV and reading and walking. Be creative in your imagination.

Convert yourself to yourself and God, or whatever your spirituality invites you to embrace. Be still.

Living will

I am struck by the number of people my age and younger who die. As I read the obituaries in the papers, I realize that several of them died from a heart attack or stoke. I imagine that most of them were unprepared to die, since they were young or very active and likely had no inclination to plan for that sort of thing. Death visited them when it was least expected.

I have met many people, through the years, who have been faced with unexpected life-conditions because of an accident, an aneurysm, a heart attack, a stroke or a cancer and have had to face an altered future unprepared.

How many fail to take the time and be responsible enough to get their affairs in order while they are alive and well? So many families are left in tumult as a result of this "job" not being done. And it *is* a job. But a simple enough one.

How little it takes to write up a living will. Do you have one? What do you want your power of attorney to do should you suffer such an event? Who would serve you best? Who would listen to you? Who would be willing?

It is important to take these responsibilities seriously — for yourself and for those who could find themselves responsible for you. It is an act of kindness to have a conversation with your family, regarding this matter. How many families I have witnessed, ripped apart, when the wishes of the disabled relative were unknown. It is important that this matter be treated with seriousness and clarity *now*, while you can still make your wishes known.

Write the information down. Sign it and have it witnessed. It is always valuable to involve a lawyer in this.

Don't have others make decisions about your life that you could make yourself. It could be about life termination; where you would like to be housed; whom you would like to care for you; where the money is; insurance information; whom you want to see, or do not want to see ever again. I have witnessed horrible family conflicts when the unknown child or spouse showed up and claim rights to a patient and to his or her world.

This is not only an act of charity and good stewardship towards your loved ones, but towards yourself as well.

Don't wait until tomorrow comes. Do it now.

Last will and testament

A last will and testament is meant to clarify what your *will* is. It also provides an opportunity to clarify what you want to leave behind that has significance to you. While you might not have property or wealth, you certainly have much to leave behind.

You can write up your own will, in your own handwriting, following any pattern you like. As long as it is signed and witnessed, it is absolutely valid. Of course, it is always advisable to have a lawyer prepare your will with the information you provide. This is a more secure way to proceed. It is not very expensive and could save a lot of family bickering at the time of your death. You can change it in any way you want and at any time, simply by authorizing and dating everything you do.

Let a few significant people know where to find your will. Perhaps you have a safety deposit box at a bank or in the basement. Let someone know.

What you say in your will is limited only by your imagination. In addition to your will, you might want to have a document to be read at the same time as their will. Some people have even made a video or CD to be played. It is not likely the best time to produce a *shocker*, but it's your show and you can produce and direct this one any way you want. Perhaps there were some things you couldn't make clear when you were alive. This can be the opportunity to do so.

It is good to include people and projects in your will who have been especially beloved by you during your life. It is not necessary to leave money or things to people who have not been beloved by you. It would be kinder, however, to discuss some of these things with someone you trust, before you die. Some people cut family members out of their will because they failed to be faithful to them during their life. That is legitimate. But be aware how federal family law will override your wishes if these are not properly communicated in a proper will. Remember that a lawyer's overview of this is always the most prudent approach to make sure your Last Will and Testament honours *your* will!

Perhaps there is some friend in need. Perhaps there has been some community organization that would benefit from your life insurance policies or your bank savings. Perhaps you have a building to donate for a hospice, or some artwork that would enhance someone's home, or could enliven some institution's bare walls. You might have a collection of recipe books, or records or vintage hats that would benefit some group. Some friends have donated their vintage clothing to theatre companies for their productions. What a great way to leave a legacy.

You might include in your will how you want private things to be disposed of — journals, personal effects you wouldn't want your family to see or know about. Perhaps you could direct some friend to clear those things out of your home before the family gets there. Better to have it written down, since families often don't understand all your relationships. Because you generally don't know when you'll die, it is better to have these things *very* clearly spelled out before you do.

Depending on what you have amassed in your lifetime, you might need a more exhaustive will. To someone who has not had a great deal of money or property, personal items might be as important to your loved ones as money. It is better to designate things — watches, jewellery, furniture, paintings, family heirlooms — because they could be the cause of tremendous disagreement among those faced with the task of distributing your effects. Resentment can build over *things*. It is kinder to have them earmarked for this one or that. If you have the time, perhaps you could give them, little by little, to your friends, at least when you feel that you are ready to part with them. So often, people are caught unprepared and everyone has the "favourite thing" that they knew you would have wanted them to have.

I have always checked my will before a major trip. It also seems to spur me on to tidy up the house, especially my office, and to tie up any loose ends. It could be looked upon as a dress rehearsal. Try to make that a habit. It could save others a great deal of pain and aggravation in the event of your death.

Do not live as though you will not die. You will. It is part of the human living process. Be prepared on every level possible. Don't miss the opportunity to die well. You will be greatly honoured by those who love you, if you do this responsibly and with great clarity.

Funeral plans

Ade Bethune was in her seventies when I visited her Rhode Island home. She had been a pioneer in church art in the 1960s. Shortly after she arrived from Belgium as a young woman, she worked with Dorothy Day in the Catholic Worker movement in New York.

I visited her for coffee and cake in the 1970s. Her art captured a freshness and integrity that should envelop the sacred. Her home spoke volumes of who she was. Like so many Europeans who had survived the horrors of the World Wars, she lived with simplicity and integrity in her life choices and in her design — even in her coffee cake, which I remember well.

In her living room, she had a most beautiful box that looked to me like a large blanket box. It was carved and painted with symbols of faith and other symbols of great significance to her. I questioned her about it. It was stunning. She had made it herself.

Then she told me that it was her coffin. Indeed, she wasn't much bigger than a blanket box and it could hold her body. My first reaction was shock. Upon reflection, I thought it most appropriate for her to have this beautifully crafted vessel to hold her beautifully crafted body. I will never forget that visit.

♪♪♪

A few years ago, my friend Donn, a celebrated potter, gave me a cremation urn for Christmas. I plan to be cremated and he knew that. We had shared that information on one of those August nights under the stars as we were celebrating together our August birthdays.

The urn sits on the mantle in our library. Now I proudly announce that I have a "pot to be in." I treasure it. I have filled it with *pot pourri* to prepare it for the day when it will hold my ashes. It is not gruesome, but appropriate and honest. My body is here now. My body will be in another form then and will rest inside that worthy vessel.

I have made it clear in my will that I do not wish to be embalmed. My body will simply be wrapped in a white cloth and cremated. My immediate family can see me dead, but there is no need for others to do so.

It could be beneficial for you and those who are dear to you to incorporate some of these ideas into *your* preparation for *your* death. Just writing the words down can help you realize that you are talking about yourself — not some foreign reality. This is *your* death. You can own it as much as you can anything else. Or you can live in denial and never grow from the experience of responsibly preparing for the inevitable. Claiming your own death can also help you face and shape your living in a new and unencumbered manner.

A gesture that I find to be very kind is happening more and more in North America. People are going to funeral homes while they are still in good health and making funeral plans. Families are generally so grief-stricken at the time of a death that they don't know which way to turn. It is a very helpful thing to know that you have pre-planned and prepaid your funeral. I was so proud of my aunt when she told me that she had done that some months ago. We discussed what was to be done upon her death and how to proceed. Now we have nothing to do but grieve and celebrate her life in a manner she would like.

Plan your funeral. Do you want to be embalmed? Do you want a viewing? Do you want an elaborate casket or burial plot? Do you want a religious ceremony — in a church, mosque, synagogue, temple? Perhaps you would prefer to be cremated and buried directly without ceremony. Do you want a party afterwards? It is up to you to decide.

When deciding these things, it is important to realize that these rituals, these gestures that happen for a few days after your death, are mainly for those you leave behind. They need meaningful symbols and gestures to help them cope with your death (and their own deaths as well).

Many people these days plan their entire farewell. Some begin their farewell before they die with a party or gathering of some kind. One priest friend, a social activist and dynamic minister, called together a great number of people and had a farewell celebration. There were songs and prayers and food and stories. It was amazing.

What an opportunity to tie up loose ends, to enjoy for the last time, the community of faithful companions who have journeyed with you along the way. It is a sad time, indeed, but also a happy time to say "yea" to who you are with some ceremony and dignity.

My friend Sherry died a few years ago. She knew she had terminal cancer. She left behind an adoring husband and three children. All of them faced her death head on. They knew she would die and they talked about it openly. They also prepared her funeral, as a family. It was to be held in the summer campground of their Anglican diocese. There was to be a Eucharist, accompanied by lots of music and participation.

When the time came, we gathered at dusk. The casket, a simple, unstained pine box, was in the middle of the field surrounded by candles and balloons. There was a basket of felt markers on the casket and everyone was invited to write something on the box. Even little children participated. It was a stretch for me to do this, but after I did, I felt I was part of the celebration in a way I wouldn't have been otherwise. Music was playing in the background. We all gathered on the hill surrounding the casket and the bishop welcomed us. There were stories, songs and scripture readings. Even their children sang. It was a hot evening and one of our friends, in a clown costume, wandered through the crowd with a squirt bottle and "refreshed" us. It was Sherry's celebration and she had made sure we were all as much a part of it as we had been at the parties we had enjoyed in her living room. It was the same Sherry.

Following the service, we went to the lodge for sandwiches, refreshments and a "Sherry cake." At her request, her body was brought to the lodge in the casket, which had been draped in flowers by her girlfriends who had journeyed with her to the end. She was not going to allow a good party to go on without being there herself. Sherry lives on in our memory in so many ways. As we left, we were all given a photo of the family with thanks and a hug.

Most people don't bother to plan for their funeral to the extent that Sherry did. They just die. It could be good for you and yours that you plan your funeral. Be clear about what you want. Hymns, the type of liturgy, celebrants, readings. You could even prepare photos or songs that represent your life.

Thank goodness there are printed services for many to follow. Most of us fall back on old ways of doing things in times of trouble. Rituals can save us in times of desperation.

Even though there might be a memorial service for you at a later date, it is important for those who are closest to you to be able to gather and remember you immediately — or at least within the days surrounding your death. Generally, they need that.

Food and stories will likely be important for your friends. Allow some time for those things.

If you have arranged to be cremated and buried without anyone being part of that activity, find some way to help people bring them closure. The old rituals of a wake, a funeral, burial and throwing or shoveling dirt on the casket were great supports to people when that was the custom. Nowadays, too many are left hanging after a death with no supporting rituals to help them express their grief. Where once we grieved publicly with black dresses and arm-bands, blinds pulled and wreaths on doors, and withdrawal from the public, now we return to work the next day as though nothing had happened. *Something happened.* And of great significance. You are gone from sight. You can help many people by planning well.

Spirituality

I am, as Tom Harpur says, an uncomfortable Christian. Christianity is the wallpaper of my life. I certainly have bathed in the deep and generous ways that Jesus of Nazareth proposed for *being* in the realm of the divine. I appreciate the legacy of his energy and compassion. He is an inspiration for my life and a true fellow traveller on the journey to fullness to which all humanity, I believe, is called.

The manner in which the churches have lived out the message of Jesus, at times leaves many in our generation baffled. A community, its rituals and its inherent energy are meant to aid us on our journey. Many find them to be beneficial. Others do not find them compelling or helpful. In the end, it is one's own synthesis of belief that will shape a way of living out one's living as well as one's dying.

The kind of living out of faith that the fundamentalist communities envision does not appeal to me. My personality has never been one that is inclined toward religious *excitement*. Culturally, my inclination directs me to a happy dance of belief, reason and imagination. Constant joy and total belief are not an acceptable stance for me. My worldview does not allow for anything that looks like a straight line.

My faith journey has led me to trust in the divine, but it has never been an easy and unquestioning process. I have experienced what I perceive as the *absence* of God, as much as I have ever experienced the *presence* of God. To me, this does not at all seem inconsistent with the faith experience of Jesus of Nazareth. Abandonment is as valid a feeling as is the utter embrace of the divine. I have experienced both. I am more aware of the sense of absence. "My God, my God, why have you abandoned me?" A familiar cry.

Teresa of Avila was a deep mystic — a nun in the Carmelite Order in the 1500s. She experienced what was called *a dark night of the soul.* Absence of God was a major theme in her contemplative and highly engaged life — for most of her life. She was realistic about faith. When a nun would approach her to tell of her amazing visions of the divine, Teresa would encourage her to "go and eat something."

I lived with the Trappist monks in Dubuque, Iowa for four months after my ordination. I thought I was called to a more contemplative existence than what the Dominican Order offered me, and fled to this Abbey. I asked one of the monks I most admired what it was like to feel the presence of God all the time and to live in the joy that would accompany that feeling. He looked at me with a smile on his face and said, "I haven't felt anything like that for twenty years!" He continued on and told me that he *simply trusted*.

Do I have a strong belief that God is on the other side of the curtain? That there will be a new world open up for me in death? That all will be calm and bright one day?

Not really. I have a trust that there is *more*. I trust that the beliefs of so many millions of us about fulfillment, reunion, communion, lasting peace and freedom from sorrow and pain will exist in some manner. I have absolutely no idea what that will be like.

I have always had a deep belief that I dwell *within* the divine. I have never believed that the divine will deliver me from the humanity I embrace, or from the joys and passions that an "earth creature" experiences. I trust that the divine energy that surrounds me, and with which I am infused, will be with me on *this*, perhaps my final journey.

Will there be more incarnations? I do not know. My faith tradition hasn't shed its imagination on that. Other traditions of belief have done so. Does it matter? Not to me. I have grown in trust. As I trust the chair on which I'm sitting, I trust in the nature of the energy that forms me.

Did Jesus, Siddhartha, or Mohammed and friends live without doubt or have clarity around their destiny? I doubt it. Their followers might claim that they did. But I doubt it. They were human, were they not?

No one can choose the path for any other human being. Each of us can become aware of various paths to spiritual health. No one path is "the one and only way." Personality, family history and culture can present many ways to us. Some stir up our imagination at one point of our life. Others, at another point. There are many aspects of our being. There are many ways to ensure health in them. Try not to close doors. There are many mansions with many possible treasures in them. They are worth exploring.

We are all on a path. Obscured … but still a path.

Forgiveness

There is an underground river that flows

deeper than remorse through the bottomland
of our lives into the valley of sorrow, carrying
our tears toward the ocean. And some of us
are left with wounds unhealed, loves
unrequited, understanding not achieved.

— *Robert Raines, A Time to Live*

It is not surprising to me that I conclude this book with reflections on forgiveness. I believe that this is the most difficult human action. Everything else pales in comparison. I have never met a human being who has not been scarred. It is part of what goes on when we live through many years on this planet. Life after mid-life seems to magnify the good times and the bad. This is the best opportunity to transform yourself into a forgiving human.

In my experience, people either take this step towards compassionate living, or they become hardened and bitter.

As I age, I find that there are deeper things to forgive and be forgiven for than when I was younger. Perhaps they develop an urgency because I know that there is not much time to reconcile those things that are loose ends in my life-knitting.

Get to know the things that haunt you. Phantoms become bigger than life when they are not named. In the process of *exorcism*, it is imperative to get the demon's correct name. So it is in the process of shriving oneself. Get words, images, smells, sounds and feelings for the items you want to deal with. The better you can describe the event or person, the better you will be able to do your *work* around them.

If you have unfinished business, pull out pictures, journals, even gifts you have received from the people you need to work on. Then put them to rest. When you do this, you can forgive them if they have harmed you. If you are not able to get to that point, at least strive to reach the point where you *want to want to forgive them.* In some cases, that might be as far as you can get at this time. It is a beginning … and a good one.

Sometimes it is possible to contact the person who has offended you, or whom you have offended. You must decide whether it is worth the energy, or whether you would be best to do your work on your own. In some cases, the person is dead or in a distant place. Perhaps they are not in your life any longer. But their image still haunts you.

Say *out loud* whatever the issue is. It is important to proclaim it, either to yourself — with your voice or with a pen — or to another. As in the case of therapy, it is imperative to be able to identify and name the issue. So it is in the art of forgiveness. Otherwise, you lose good energy that could help you heal.

There are some things you can clean up. There are others that might linger on — either because the wounds are so deep, or the person is still on the screen in your life.

Pray for them. Ask that they be fine. Don't wish them harm. This may be very difficult for you to do. They have likely lived through enough pain, as well — just because they are human. No hatred directed towards them will help either them or you. Praying for them will change you, first of all, and then, could have some effect on them.

In my experience with people, I have found that it is not the other with which we have the greatest difficulty. Usually, it is ourselves. Some of us have a terrible time getting over the things we did and said that have deepened our regret or shame. These regrets, or shame scripts, are powerful enough to block out happiness and contentment in our lives.

This toxicity does not just invade our thoughts. It inhabits our whole person. Just as grief is never simply a state of mind, regret, shame and hatred also impregnate our total ecosystem. Thus, it is not possible to detoxify, forgive or forget by simply doing mind or talk-work.

Fasting with the purpose of clearing your heart-screen can be a most beneficial activity. Walking, lifting weights, chopping wood, scrubbing the kitchen floor, knitting, working on a puzzle, singing, dancing with vigour, screaming — all of these things can help you re-balance and forgive — if they are done with intention.

You might even invite a friend for a meal and after talking about the blockage or sadness that inhabits you, eat for reconciliation. The peace that follows could be a great blessing.

You might do a scouring of your home in order to change the energy. You could decide to move, leave town, take a vacation, change your name or reclaim your birth name.

It is hard to forgive. Jesus of Nazareth says forgive seventy times seventy times. Often it takes that long. Just don't forget that sad energy can never be dissolved without expression.

Exhale your bad breath. Inhale fresh new energy.

And never forget to forgive yourself … again … and again … and again … and again …

Conclusion

At the dawn of the twenty-first century, humankind is faced with the age-old struggle between agony and ecstasy. We live in a time that is fueled by fear. Fear of venturing into an unknown future, fear of new untried models for international cooperation, fear of new styles of living *family,* and fear of the use of imagination as we seek a spirituality that fits our new world.

Nations, leaders and individuals have a choice. Either we embrace the future with trust, solidarity and conversation, or we cower, hide and rage against the unknown, in toxicity, protectionism and war. This is not new to us. The slippery snake of terrorism, which grows out of fear, has reared its ugly head at each major paradigm shift in the story of humankind. Now, we have reached that exact point once again in human growth. We have shifted. We are there!

Many in our generation are willing to live with the solutions to the eternal questions that were formulated in the Middle Ages, or in the nineteenth century. They live with the illusion that answers from times past could work for us. Others are willing to live with imagination and trust — they are anxious to forge new ways of growing. A life fueled by rage and fear produces rage, shame and control. Only life fueled by love and imagination can blossom positively.

We can best grow by understanding, from history, how civilizations have broken through the dilemma brought about naturally by growth. What insights did they have that allowed them to move into new models of living? Slavish adherence to old solutions never generates fresh responses to the issues that arise in every generation. How can we move forward? Life is never static. It always calls for change and growth.

Amor vincit omnia. Love conquers all. These words, which were proclaimed in the Canterbury Tales in the Middle Ages, are true for this pilgrimage in the twenty-first century.

The Jesuit "geologian," Teilhard de Chardin, suggested that we are now growing in the *neosphere*, or the reign of mind and love. He suggested that we have grown out of survival mode and are entering into a new creative time for humanity. Witness the growth in our lifetime as the psychological era pulled us out of the toxicity of fear and abuse, which we inherited from our forbears.

There is, indeed, more health today than there was yesterday. There is more promise for us in the future, than in the past, if we choose love over hatred, imagination over formula. We must make a choice for love.

We elders are a strong force for the future of humankind. As a group we can inspire, educate, prod and encourage as we help the next generation design how to live in this world in such a way that everyone has a right to fullness. That cannot be done by embracing fear. That only produces division and war. Love produces radiance, peace and joy. It dignifies diversity, change and imagination.

This dream for humankind cannot be realized without personal conversion. These pages have been written with this dream in mind. Live in truth, integrity and justice. Become more and more expansive as you grow old. Be generous with whatever you have and never be afraid to share the gift of your being with the next generation.

Grow somewhere. Water your garden with tears of sadness and joy. Embrace tomorrow with love.

Acknowledgments

Much wisdom, experience and good old-fashioned friendship have made this book a living organism. Thanks to:

Ray Harsant, who has read, re-read and challenged page after page and been the friend that every writer needs.

Morgan, our beloved Nova Scotia Duck Tolling Retriever, who lived through these pages and then left us for dog heaven. He still lives at Ash Croft in so many ways.

Judy Anderson, who edited, typeset, designed and encouraged me throughout the entire process.

Deb and Brian Usher at Arabella Pines, who photographed and designed the cover and more than that, shared with me the business and adventure of books.

Michael Lavelle, who always trusted my life choices and allowed me to be an honoured elder for generations of his students at Erindale College, University of Toronto.

Fulvio Cubello, my personal trainer, who helps me grow to be a fit and joyful elder.

George Black, friend, colleague, anchor, who died as he lived — with dignity, grace and delight. And his wife Mags, who still dances with him.

Neighbours, some of whom are not old enough to be my elders, who have shown me that life can be wonderful — Pat and Bob Martin, Camille and Pat Hodgson, Laura and Jeff Ryan, Dwight Caldwell and Kim Zammit, Siobhan Dempsey and Maurice Byrne (my techno-saviour) and the deer, wild turkeys, fox, coyotes and yes, even the squirrels and chipmunks, not to mention those skunks, raccoons and porcupines. And the flowers and grasses and trees and the sparkling white and pink and blue snows that cushion our days and fill the nights with sweet sounds.

New friends on the journey who came for the *Growing Somewhere* series of workshops here at Ash Croft over the past four years as well as those brave souls who come here for longer retreats, sharing wisdom, stories, good food and music.

And all those who have died and left this fragile island home, our mother earth. May they have laughter without end.

Bibliography

James Agee, *A Death in the Family.* New York: Bantam Books, 1982.

Mitch Albom, *Tuesdays With Morrie: An old man, a young man, and life's greatest lesson.* New York: Doubleday, 1997.

Lisa Appignanesi, *Kicking Fifty.* Toronto: McArthur & Company, 2003.

Karen Armstrong, *A Battle for God, a History of Fundamentalism.* New York: Ballantine Books, 2000.

Katherine Ashenburg, *The Mourner's Dance. What we do when people die.* Toronto: MacFarlane, Walter and Ross, 2002.

Ernest Becker, *The Denial of Death.* New York: Macmillan, 1975.

Thomas Berry, *The Dream of the Earth*. San Francisco: Sierra Books, 1988.

Julia Blackburn, *Daisy Bates in the Desert: A woman's life among the Aborigines*. New York: Pantheon Books, 1994.

Frederick Buechner, *The Sacred Journey.* New York: Harper and Row,1982.

Robert Butler and Myrna Lewis, *Love and Sex After Sixty.* New York: Harper and Row, 1976.

John Cheever, *The Journals of John Cheever.* New York: Ballantine, 1991.

Mantak Chia and Douglas Abrams, *The Multi-Orgasmic Male: Sexual secrets every man should know.* San Francisco: Harper San Francisco, 1996.

James Clarke, *The Ancient Pedigree of Plums*. Toronto: Exile Editions, 1999.

Gene Cohen, *The Creative Age: Awakening human potential in the second half of life*. New York: Quill, 2001.

Pat Conroy, *The Prince of Tides*. New York: Bantam Books, 1986.

Pat Conroy, *Beach Music*. New York: Bantam Books, 1995.

Ram Dass, *Still Here: Embracing aging, changing and dying.* New York: Riverhead Books, 2002.

Ken Dychtwald, *Age Power: How the 21st Century will be ruled by the New Old.* Putnam, 1999.

Timothy Findley, *Dust to Dust: Stories*. Toronto: Harper Collins, 1997.

Richard Florida, *The Rise of the Creative Class: How it's transforming work, leisure, community and everyday life*. New York: Perseus Books, 2002.

Matthew Fox, *The Coming of the Cosmic Christ.* New York: Harper and Row, 1988.

Matthew Fox, *Creation Spirituality: Liberating gifts for the peoples of the earth.* San Francisco: Harper Collins, 1991.

Matthew Fox, *The Re-invention of Work.* San Francisco: Harper Collins, 1994.

Betty Friedan, *The Fountain of Age.* New York: Simon and Shuster, 1993.

Jean Giono, *The Man Who Planted Trees.* Chelsea, VT: Chelsea Green Publishing Company, 1985.

Marlene Halpin, *Forgiving, Present Perfect.* Dubuque: W.C. Brown Co., 1987.

Tom Harpur, *Life After Death.* Toronto: McLelland & Stewart, 1999 .

Tom Harpur, *Would You Believe? Finding God Without Losing Your Mind.* Toronto: McLelland & Stewart, 1996.

Troon Harrison and Eugenie Fernandes, *Lavender Moon.* Toronto: Annick Press, 1997.*

Carolyn Heilbrun, *The Last Gift of Time: Life Beyond Sixty.* New York: Ballantine Books, 1997.

James Hillman, *The Force of Character and the Lasting Life.* New York: Random House, 1999.

Richard Horne, *101 Things to do Before you Die.* London: Bloomsbury, 2005.

Jane Jacobs, *The Nature of Economies.* New York: Random House, 2000.

Jane Jacobs, *Dark Ages Ahead, Caution.* New York: Random House, 2004.

Norman Jewison, *This Terrible Business Has Been Good to Me: An autobiography.* Toronto: Key Porter, 2004.

Sandy Johnson and Dan Budnik, *The Book of Elders, The Life Stories and Wisdom of Great American Indians.* San Francisco: Harper Collins, 1994.

Anodea Judith, *Wheels of Life, A User's Guide to the Chakra System.* St. Paul: Llewellyn Press, 1989.

Carl Jung, *Psychological Reflections: A new anthology of his writings*. London: J. Jacobi, 1971.

Gershan Kaufman, *Shame, The Power of Caring.* Rochester VT: Shenkman, 1985.

Gershan Kaufman and Lev Raphael, *Coming Out Of Shame.* New York: Doubleday, 1996.

Nikos Kazantzakis, *Report to Greco.* London: Faber & Faber, 1965.

Nikos Kazantzakis, *Zorba the Greek.* New York, Simon and Shuster, 1952.

Sam Keen, *The Passionate Life: Stages of Loving.* New York: Bantam, 1983.

Sam Keen, *Fire in the Belly: On being a man.* New York: Bantam Books, 1991.

Sam Keen, *Inward Bound: Exploring the geography of your emotions.* New York: Bantam Books, 1992.

Allan Kellehear, *Grief and Remembering: 25 Australians tell it like it is.* Melbourne: Riivoli, 2001.

Hans Kung, *Eternal Life? Life after Death as a Medical, Philosophical and Theological Problem, translation Edward Quinn.* Garden City, NY: Doubleday & Co, 1984.

Frances Moore Lappé and Jeffrey Perkins, *You Have the Power: Choosing courage in a culture of fear.* New York: Tarcher/Penguin, 2004.

Michael Lawlor, *Earth Honoring: The New Male Sexuality.* Rochester, VT: Park Street Press, 1989.

Denis Ledoux, *Turning Memories into Memoirs: A handbook for writing life stories.* Lisbon Falls, Maine: Soleil Press, 1993.

Denis Ledoux, The Photo Scribe: How to write the stories behind the photographs. Lisbon Falls, Maine: Soleil Press, 1999.

Stephen Levine, *Who Dies? An Investigation of Conscious Living and Conscious Dying.* New York: Doubleday, 1982.

Daniel Levinson, *The Seasons of a Man's Life.* New York: Alfred A. Knopf, 1978.

Chris Maser, The Redesigned Forest. Toronto: Stoddart, 1990.

Neil McKenty, *The Inside Story: Journey of a former Jesuit Priest and Talk Show Host Towards Self-Discovery.* Ste-Anne de Bellevue, QC: Shoreline, 1997.

John A.B. McLeish, *The Challenge of Aging — Ulyssean Paths to Creative Living.* Toronto, 1983.

Thomas Merton, *Seven Story Mountain*. New York: Harcourt, 1999.

Alice Miller,*The Drama of the Gifted Child.* New York: Meridian, 1983.

Alice Miller, *For Your Own Good: Hidden cruelty in child rearing and the roots of violence.* New York: Meridian, 1983.

Alice Miller, *Thou Shalt Not Be Aware: Society's betrayal of the child.* New York: Meridian, 1986.

Alice Miller, *The Untouched Key: Tracing childhood trauma in creativity.* New York: Doubleday, 1990.

Barbara Moses, *What Next? The Complete Guide to Taking Control of your Work Life.* Toronto: DK Publishing, 2003.

Alice Munro, *Hateship, Friendship, Courtship, Loveship, Marriage.* Toronto: McClelland and Stewart, 2001.

David Moberg, ed., *Aging and Spirituality: Spiritual Dimensions of Aging Theory, Research, Practice and Policy.* New York: The Haworth Pastoral Press, 2001.

Robert Munsch, *Love You Forever.* Willowdale: Firefly Press,1986.*

Henri Nouwen and Walter Gaffney, *Aging: The Fulfillment of Life.* New York: Doubleday, 1976.

David W. Opheim, *The Teachings of Jaysos: An earthly approach to a spiritual way of life.* Toronto: Pine Rock Point Creations, 1995.

Carlo Petrini, William McQuaig, John Updike, *Slow Food (The Case for Taste)*. New York: Columbia University Press, 2003.

Jane R. Pretat, *Coming to Age*. Toronto: Inner City, 1994.

Dini Petty, *The Queen, the Bear and the Bumblebee*. Vancouver: Whitecap Publishing, 2000.*

Annie Proulx, *The Shipping News*. New York: Simon and Shuster, 1993.

Robert Raines, *A Time to Live (Seven Steps to Creative Aging)*. New York: Plume Books, Penguin, 1997.

Sogyal Ripoche, *The Tibetan Book of Living and Dying*. New York: Harper Collins, 1993.

Philip Roth, *The Dying Animal*. New York: Random House, 2001.

Jonathan Sacks, *The Dignity of Difference: How to Avoid the Clash of Civilization*. London and New York: Continuum, 2002.

Zalman Schachter-Shalomi, and Ronald S. Miller, *From Aging to Sage-ing, A Profound New Vision of Growing Older.* New York: Warner Books, 1995.

Johnathan Schell, *The Fate of the Earth*. London: Johnathan Cape, 1982

Martin Seligman, *Authentic Happiness: Using the New Positive Psychology to Realize your Potential for Lasting Fulfillment*. New York: Free Press, 2002.

Gail Sheehy, *New Passages.* New York: Random House, 1995.

Marsha Sinetar, *Ordinary People as Monks and Mystics.* New York: Paulist Press, 1986.

Marti Smye, *Is It Too Late To Run Away and Join The Circus?* Toronto: Key Porter Books, 1998.

Dorothee Soelle and Shirley A. Cloyes, *To Work and to Love. A Theology of Creation.* Philadelphia: Fortress Press, 1984.

Thich Nhat Hanh, *Peace Is Every Step: The Path of Mindfulness in Everyday Life.* New York: Bantam Books, 1991.

Pierre Teilhard de Chardin, *The Future of Man.* New York: Harper and Row, 1964.

Eckhart Tolle, *The Power of Now.* Vancouver: Namaste Publishing Inc., 1997.

Sally Vickers, *Instances of the Number 3.* London: Harper Collins, 2001.

Judith Viorst, *Necessary Losses.* New York: Ballantine, 1986.

Margaret Visser, *The Rituals of Eating.* New York: Grove, 1992.

Kelly Walker, *Loss of Soul: Burnout.* Rosemont, ON: KW Productions, 1997.

Kelly Walker, *Dancing on the Ark: Facing Change in Uncertain Times.* Rosemont, ON: KW Productions, 2000.

Fred Warshovsky, *Stealing Time: The New Science of Aging.* New York: TV Books, 1999.

Dwight Lee Wolter, *Forgiving Our Parents.* Minneapolis: CompCare, 1989.

Marion Woodman, *Bone: Dying into Life.* New York: Viking Press, 2004.

Orvin D. Yalom, *When Nietzsche Wept.* New York: Harper Collins, 1992.

Carol Zaleski and Philip Zaleski, eds., *The Book of Heaven.* Oxford: University Press, 2000.

* Recommended for children as well as adults

Web Sites of Interest

- **www.50plus.com** (Canadian Association of Retired Persons).
- **www.aarp.org** (American Association of Retired Persons).
- **www.ilcusa.org** (The International Longevity Center, USA. Human Values in Aging Newsletter).
- **www.turningmemories.com** (Denis Ledoux web site for writing memoirs).
- **www.donnzver.com** Donn Zver Pottery.
- **www.oxfordchurchmusic.ca**
- **www.elderhostel.org**
- **www.kwalker.com**

Appendix: Food for Your Journey

Eternal Spirit,
Earth-maker, Pain bearer, Life-giver,
Source of all that is and shall be,
Father and Mother of us all,
Loving God in whom is heaven.

The hallowing of your name echo through the universe!
The way of your justice be followed by the peoples of the world!
Your heavenly will be done by all created beings!
Your commonwealth of peace and freedom
Sustain our hope and come on earth.

With the bread we need for today, feed us.
In the hurts we absorb from one another, forgive us.
In times of temptation and test, strengthen us.
From trials too great to endure, spare us.
From the grip of all that is evil, free us.

For you reign in the glory of the power that is love,
Now and forever. Amen.

— *The New Zealand Prayer Book, 1989*

Becoming A Senior

Now that I'm losing my hair and nearing
The edge,
Hear death pecking at my ribs,
Beginning to dribble
In my underwear,
Certain facts are becoming clear:

I'll never ski to the North Pole,
Hand-glide off a glacier,
Or become the world's fastest yodeller;

Never win the Nobel Prize for chemistry,
Star in a Hollywood blockbuster
Or be a sumo wrestler;

Grand Chess Master, astronaut,
World champion spear thrower,
I can forget, along with
Astrophysics and the Internet;
My time-warped heart's circumscribed, I'll already
Admit, certain things will never fit.

But that's okay, I don't intend
To grumble or to sulk;
Death's an insult on all our plates
And I'll never be an ingrate to complain:
After all I'm still alive, loved
And been loved, and while
The mystic rose of contentment eludes
Me … still,

I can proclaim: I love my breath,
My sparrow light in this glade or dark, nothing to sneeze at sixty-five.

— *Judge James Clarke*

there will be a time
when tulips come
on time
and butter tarts
are served
before the lamb.

when
people dance
whatever colour or degree or sex
in robes of deepest, rich
vermillion
with veils and emeralds and frankincense
and New Spice.

for every day will then unfold
as tympanies and bells
and laughter and choirs
huge with eagles' wings
enfolding all the space
into a dance hall
of desire.

o lift us up, you eagles
and sing to us, you doves
and lead us into
giggles
and
the child.

— *Kelly Walker*

Was it autumn that came
or summer that slipped away?
Between the thunder claps
I grasped a moment's mist.
Between now and again
I touched a hand that offered me
tenderness
and security
and memories to hold on to.
But then the thunder struck again
and laughter turned to sawdust
as we collided
flesh upon flesh upon tears and forgetting.
And yellow green horizons leapt ahead.

Oh mercy on us!
cried my little voice.
As from a dream,
I mustered up the strength to call for help
from far off promises of aid
from sailors in the night

and lovers on the brink
and solemn monks with vespers in their drawers.

Don't run from me!
my voice commanded.
Get back, and do your job!
For laughter should be ours –
not lamentation now!

Listen to my voice!

— *Kelly Walker*

Living

So many years ago
I knew you wouldn't mind
I changed my name to innocent
And left my past behind

Before I knew your trembling heart
Before my sweet tears washed away
Before my life fell apart
Now it's time for a brand new day

Sweeter than the morning dew
Upon the petal rose
Warmer than the rising sun
My love for you still grows

The shifting sand beneath my feet
Has taught me how to dance

The pine trees clinging to the rocky ledge
Taught me to take a chance

The wind that blew me off the cliff
Has taught me how to fly
Who'd guess I'd really learn to live
In learning how to die.

—Carolyn Elizabeth Hafner (1959-1994)
July 14, 1993

On Death

Once upon a time, life began for twin boys in their mother's womb. The spark of life glowed until it caught fire with the formation of their embryonic brains. With life and their simple brains came feeling, and with feeling, a sense of each other, of self. When they perceived the life of each other, they knew that life was good and they laughed and rejoiced, the one saying, "Lucky are we to have this world." And the other chiming, "Blessed by the Mother who gave us this life and each other."

Each budded and grew arms and fingers, lean legs and stubby toes. They stretched their lungs, churned and turned in their new-found world. They explored their world, and in it found the life cord which gave them life from the precious Mother's blood. So they said, “How great is the love of the Mother that she shared all she has with us.”

And they were pleased and satisfied with their lot. Weeks passed into months, and with the advent of each new month, they noticed a change in themselves.

“We are changing. What can it mean? It means that we are drawing near to birth.”

An unsettling chill crept over the two, and they both feared, for they knew that birth meant leaving all their world behind.

Said the one, “Were it up to me, I would live here forever.”

“But mightn’t there be a life after birth?”

“How can there be life after birth? Do we not share our life cord and also the blood tissues? And have you ever talked to one who has been born? Has anyone re-entered the womb after birth? No!”

He fell into despair, the one stabbed the darkness with his unseeing eyes, and as he clutched his precious life cord to his chest, he said, “If all this is so and life is absurd, then there can really be no Mother.”

“But there is a Mother, who else gave us our nourishment and our world?”

"We get our own nourishment and our world has always been here. And if there is a Mother, where is she? Have you ever seen her? Does she ever talk to you? We invented Mother because it satisfied a need in us. It makes us feel secure and happy."

Thus, while one raved and despaired, the other resigned himself to birth, and placed his trust into the hands of the Mother. Hours ached into days and days fell into weeks and it became time. Both knew their death was at hand, and both feared what they did not know. As the one was the first to be conceived, so he was the first to be born, the other following after.

They cried as they were born to the light, and coughed out fluid and gasped in the dry air. And when they were sure they had been born, they opened their eyes for the first time, and found themselves cradled in the warm love of the Mother. They lay open-mouthed, awe-struck before the one they could only hope to know.

— *Craig Boly, S.J.*